Dedicated by

**Raymond and
Elizabeth Gindi**

in honor of

**Al and
Shirley Gindi**

THE KEY TO A SUCCESSFUL LIFE

By

Rabbi David Bassous

Contents	Page

Preface 5

1. The Mystery of Life 7

2. Purpose 29

3. Free Will 53

4. Human Personality 65

5. Sin & Guilt 93

6. Accountability 97

7. The Teshuvah Process 125

8. Success 143

9. Perfection 163

10. The "Quick Reference Guide" to Inner Peace 173

11. Glossary 177

Preface

Because of the rapid pace of life today and the high level of stress that is prevalent in the workplace, we are witnessing a tremendous interest in various self-help manuals that offer quasi-psychological insights. Modern man is looking to find self-esteem, confidence and social harmony in the framework of a fast-paced technological society. Unbeknown to many, Jewish texts have a lot to say on this most pressing current issue. This volume consists of a brief guide on achieving some measure of contentment and satisfaction in our relationship with God, fellowman and within ourselves, and some guidance and mussar (ethics) on how a person should approach and live life with purpose and a continual striving for success and perfection.

I thank the Almighty for granting me a portion among those who study His Torah and the ability to learn, teach and perform the mitzvot.

I wish to acknowledge all the love, care and nurturing I received from my beloved parents. I am indebted to my dear father of blessed memory who imbued us with love of Hashem and His Torah, my dear mother who drilled into us a moral compass, may she live many more healthy and happy years.

I thank from the bottom of my heart all my teachers and the institutions of learning that I attended, who strengthened my avodat Hashem, *chizku ve'imtzu*, may Hashem bless you all millions of times over for what you have given me.

My precious wife Clara has been a pillar of strength in all my undertakings, despite our moving from place to place across the globe. Like Rabbi Akiva's wife Rachel, she willingly sacrificed her time with me when I was away learning and teaching. She is a true *eshet hayil*. I appreciate her self-sacrifice and

devotion, may Hashem reward her millions of times over and may she witness many generations of dorot yesharim emanate from her.

My dear in-laws, Shem Tov, alav hashalom, and Rachel Benmergui, may she live many more healthy and happy years, who warmly accepted me like a son into their hearts, and all their children and progeny.

My brothers and sister, their spouses and families, and their children and grandchildren, thank you for your support.

I send my warmest greetings to all my delightful friends and congregants at Congregation Etz Ahaim, with much appreciation for your friendship and encouragement in all my endeavors.

I thank Hashem for my dear children: Shlomo, Rabbi Yonatan and Hefsi, Rabbi Yitzchak and Esther, Rachel and Rabbi David, Miriam and Rabbi Yosef, Yoseph and Chana and all my beloved grandchildren. May Hashem bless you all with much hatzlachah ubrachah and growth.

Special thanks to **Pinny Cohen** for his design of the cover and encouragement to complete this project.

Finally I wish to thank **Raymond & Elizabeth Gindi** for dedicating this book in honor of **Al & Shirley Gindi**.

Please Hashem, grant peace and security to Your faithful nation Israel, who despite thousands of years of exile, persecution and deprivation still learn Your Torah and keep Your mitzvot. 'Uba lesion goel…'

Rabbi David Bassous,
Tishri 5776

Chapter 1. The Mystery of Life

With all the recent advances made in science and knowledge, mankind is still baffled by the mysteries of life. Where did we come from? Are we the only rational beings in the universe? Why did God create us? What is our purpose?

With the advent of modern technology like gigantic radio telescopes and other sophisticated devices, we have begun to appreciate the vastness of space. For thousands of years, ancient man had no inkling of what lay beyond his field of vision, but the Bible (Torah) insight-fully told us that there is more than meets the eye.

Three times God promised Abraham that his progeny would be numerous. The first time, in Genesis 13:16, He promised that "they would be as numerous as the specks of earth in the ground." The second time (Genesis 15:5), He pledged that they would be "as numerous as the stars in the sky." The third time (Genesis 22:17), He promised that they will be as numerous "as the stars in the sky and grains of sand by the seashore."

To the naked eye on a clear night only about 6,000 stars are visible. Abraham and others who lived prior to the invention of the telescope must have wondered what kind of a comparison this was. How could God contrast the six thousand or so stars to the trillions of specks of earth and sand? Today, thanks to modern technology, we can understand this equation.[1] There is no way any ancient writer could have made such a blatantly unequal comparison.

How do we fit into this immense and complex picture? Are we important? Do we matter? Do we have free will? Is there a Creator?

---

[1] Interestingly, an average handful of sand contains approximately six thousand grains, or the number of stars visible on a clear night to the naked eye. Today we know that there are many more stars in the universe than grains of sand on our planet.

Mystery excites and tantalizes us, hence the popularity of mystery books and movies. By comparison, how much thought do we put into the mystery of our existence? The universe tantalizes us with mysteries but we choose instead to focus on man-made, trivial, counterfeit mysteries, like those created by writers and portrayed in movies and television. Isn't it sad that we choose to ignore the most fundamental and important mysteries of all? We should ask how, why and what-for questions about our very existence!

The complexity and vastness of the universe gives us a small glimpse into the greatness of our Creator. Our monotheistic religion started with such a question. This was the way that Abraham, our ancestor, came to appreciate God.[2] Post-biblical writers further speak of God's existence, and of humankind's ability to gain awareness. Maimonides[3] also known as Rambam, explains, in the laws dealing with the prohibitions of idolatrous practice (Avodat Kochavim) 1:3, that Abraham pondered the existence of the universe and came to the rational and logical conclusion that the universe must have a Creator.

Rambam's son, Rabbi Abraham, in his introduction to the Eyn Yaakov,[4] lists two ways to gain awareness of God: The first way is through observing His creations: When a person takes a walk in the forest, or along the beach or on the mountains, or on beholding any grand natural vista, he or she should be awed by God's handiwork and be drawn closer to Him. The second way is through learning Torah and appreciating the truths, deep wisdom and goodness inherent in God's manual for human living.

---

[2] The Bible credits Abraham with the re-emergence of ethical monotheism.

[3] One of the greatest Torah scholars of all time, see glossary at the end of the book.

[4] A multi-volume work consisting of stories and parables of the Talmud.

The Wonders of Creation, - The Human Body

To obtain a better feeling for the complexity of creation, let us examine the human body: its miles and miles of tubing (veins, arteries, and intestines) its miles of electrical circuitry (nerves and hundreds of thousands of connections of the nervous system). Just think of how many nerves go through the spinal column! The muscles that make the bones move are triggered by tiny electrical impulses relayed from the brain and delivered via the nervous system.

The body has a thermostat to adjust its climate control system. It has a tremendous self-healing apparatus and a defense mechanism against bacteria and sickness. Think of the body's ability to obtain energy and nutrition from its surroundings, utilizing complex chemical reactions!

The body never really ceases its activity. Day and night, it is busy, constructing new cells, warding off illness, processing nutrients, and orchestrating a host of physical and biochemical actions, all of which contribute to health and a sense of well-being.

The human brain is like a small and powerful computer, which controls all mental, emotional and physical functions, most without any conscious thought. The brain is able to interpret and react to all incoming information within milliseconds, even without a person having to deliberately focus and think. Attempts to construct devices that mimic its operation have been unsuccessful.

Those with even casual knowledge of biology or the other natural sciences are well aware that nature's level of complexity far surpasses the complexity exhibited by an object with right angles and smooth surfaces. Let us appreciate this. An embryology textbook, From Conception to Birth, asks honest questions about the human brain and its nervous system. How do the billions of cells comprising this system come into being in the first place, the textbook asks, and how do they attach themselves to each other to form a network connecting the brain to every muscle, organ and gland in the entire body? How is it possible for microscopic chromosomes, each containing all the coded information necessary to produce and "wire" an entire human being, to have come into existence without a designer?

It would be relatively easy to understand if the neurons were connected to the brain like spokes of a wheel, but they are not. Most of these neurons are connected to a great many other neurons; one estimate is that, on the average, each neuron is connected with one thousand others. This means a total of ten trillion connections. A complete wiring diagram of this network would stagger the imagination. All of the telephone cables of the world would comprise no more than a small fraction of it.

The neuron, like any other cell, contains a nucleus that is identical to those in the original fertilized egg. Thus the nucleus of each neuron contains a catalog of potentiality inherited genes from both mother and father. How can a collection of genes possibly account for the multifarious connections between neurons and the human nervous system? How can a collection of genes possibly account for the relationship between neurons, muscles and organs of the body? There are only approximately forty thousand genes in all the chromosomes, seemingly not enough to encode instructions for performing ten trillion connections.

But if every last interconnection is not spelled out in the chromosomes then how do the neurons get connected? Do they just reach out for one another haphazardly? Obviously not, since all neurons fulfill definite, specialized functions, not random ones. Connections between the nerves associated with hearing and those controlling, say, the biceps muscles wouldn't be logical or effective, and above all, the nervous system effectively coordinates whatever the person does or thinks.

The nervous system eventually comprises the most efficient cable system in the world for the transmission of messages. Ultimately, each nerve fiber will be covered by a sheath of protective cells (sometimes five thousand per fiber) and each will be able to carry messages at a speed of three hundred miles per hour. From these primitive cells, first distinguishable a few days after conception, the embryo will form more than ten thousand taste buds in its mouth.

Some twelve million nerve endings will form the baby's nose to help it to detect fragrances or odors in the air. More than one hundred thousand nerve cells will be devoted to reacting to Beethoven's Fifth Symphony or the ticking of a Swiss watch. The piano has only two hundred and forty strings, but the baby's ears will have over two hundred and forty thousand hearing units to detect the smallest variations in sound.

The baby's eyes, which begin to form at nineteen days, will have more than twelve million screen points per square centimeter. The retina, or light-sensitive portion of its eye, will have more than fifty billion such points. The composite picture the eyes record is homogeneous, because the information collected by these light-sensitive points is blended into a whole. Take a hand lens and examine any picture in any daily newspaper. You will find it made up of hundreds of points, each light or dark, which together make up the picture as you look at it from a greater distance. This is exactly what the eye does, only in much finer detail.

Where do these billions of cells in the nervous system come from? From the original ovum, this is still dividing after one month to form the tissues and organs that the child requires. It has been estimated that all two billion of the specific nerve cells which make any individual educable are located in the outer covering of his brain, its cortex, and that these two billion cells could be stored in a thimble.

Development continues in certain parts of the brain, even after birth. By the end of the first month of embryonic development, none of these parts of the brain, spinal nerves or sense organs, is completely formed, but the foundation for all of them has been laid.

The textbook[5] does not mention the word, God, but it states:

> "The development of the brain and nervous system and its rule of the integration of all the systems is one of the most profound mysteries of embryology. The eyes alone display such intelligent planning as to stupefy anyone studying them. They are formed on the sides of the head and are ready for connection to the optic nerves growing out independently from the brain. The forces that ensure this integration have thus far not been discovered, but they must be formidable indeed, since more than one million optic nerve fibers must mesh with each eye. Think for a moment about what is considered to be a feat of human engineering: the drilling of tunnels from both sides of the Alps that must somehow meet precisely and merge into one continuous highway. Yet any one of the thousands of things the fetus must do as part of the routine of development is far more wondrous."

The eyes are a tremendously complex three-dimensional camera. First, light hits the lenses of the eye, which focuses the light. The light then passes through the pupil, then through the colorless liquid inside the eyeball, to hit the retina located at the back of the eyeball.[6]

---

[5] From Conception to Birth; Lipson, Tony (Millenia Books) 1994.

[6] The retina contains amazingly complex nerve cells called rods and cones. Rods are specialized for dim light, whereas cones are important for color vision and sharpness. The light is received by the rods and cones and turned into an electrical signal. This electrical signal is passed to the bipolar cells and then to a bundle of nerve fibers called the optic nerve.

The retina receives all information upside down and backwards. This information is then transmitted to the back of the brain. All the visual information from the right side of space is sent to the left side or hemisphere of the brain. Visual information from the left side of space is transmitted to the right side of the brain. Virtually the entire brain is wired 'backwards and upside down' so that the visual information, which comes in 'backwards and upside down,' can be dealt with efficiently.

Imagine that you see a fly coming at you from the left. This visual information is sent within milliseconds to the back of the right hemisphere. The information is processed and analyzed subconsciously or consciously. Your brain analyzes all the information and within a second you may decide to swat the fly.

We take for granted the amazing visual system that we have been given. It is among the most complex systems known to science. It is so complex that some scientists have argued that evolution alone could not account for such a wondrous system. Hence, the visual system points to a Creator.

There are more complex neural systems that deal with intangible activities like the ability to remember and to forget.

Human emotions, what triggers them and where they are located in the brain, are subjects of ongoing research. Modern research is focusing on the effects of chemical imbalances on the mind and the possibility that many "emotional disorders" have a chemical origin.

There are many things concerning the brain that remain unknown, and to a great extent the workings of the mind remain a mystery. For instance, what causes a person who has been in a coma for seven years to suddenly awaken? This recently occurred to an American police officer. He remembered events that took place seven years earlier with clarity, as if they had just happened.

This is very similar to the story in the Talmud (Taanit 23a) about Choni Hamaagel. The Talmud states that Choni went to sleep and awoke seventy years later and found the town he had lived in totally changed. Note that Jewish belief has always posited that the difference between a person in a coma and a normal person has to do with the soul and the measure of its presence or absence. The Talmud in Berachot 57b mentions that sleep is one sixtieth of death.

More recently, Rabbi Suleiman Sassoon of blessed memory[7] once said that the whole world will come to believe in God when scientists will discover the soul. Through this discovery humanity will come to a realization of the Divine. Then, "the world will be spread with knowledge of God just like water covers the seas." (Isaiah 11, 9)

Faith and Healing

There is an awakening happening in the midst of this high-tech world in which we live. People are becoming cognizant of the fact that we have a spiritual component as well as a physical body and the fact that they both need attention. They are learning to nurture this inner spirit through the forgotten power of meditation and prayer. Simple acts of faith are mocked by modern society. Yet belief is the antidote to confusion and hopelessness, and without it a person will collapse in the face of life's inequities. Life's unfairness and ugliness are all around us, ready to drag us down. Belief is the means by which we do not let external circumstances control our inner lives. It is the way to maintain our personal strength in the midst of adversity.[8]

---

[7] Noted contemporary scholar, author, philanthropist and philosopher, and one of the most humble people this author has ever met.

[8] Intellect and reason alone are not enough to solve the complex problems we face today. Even now there are courses in faith and medicine in 30 of our country's medical schools. This is good news. It is truly an exciting time to see modern aspects of healing embrace ageless spiritual truths.

Prayer is the means by which we connect to a power higher than ourselves to reaffirm our own inner abilities. This can lead us to contentment regardless of circumstances, and enable us to combat the negative forces in our environment.

Many articles have been written about the mind-body connection. People who live with constant anger, resentment and bitterness affect their health adversely by triggering damaging stress hormones. What affects us most are the words we say to ourselves. The impact of our thoughts can be measured by changes in heart rate, muscle tension, blood pressure and respiration. We can literally harm our bodies and slow down the healing process of an illness with negative internal messages. Alternatively, to assert that there is hope when everything looks dark may appear naïve but it is the kind of positive illusion that is generated by faith.

One of the best documented studies on the effect of prayer on healing was conducted in 1988 by a cardiologist, Dr. Herbert Benson, and his partner Dr. Richard Friedman.[9] Over a 10-month period, 393 patients in the coronary unit were randomly assigned to receive or not to receive prayer by complete strangers. The patients who received daily prayer had fewer complications and life threatening situations such as pneumonia and cardiopulmonary events (See Science Vol. 276, 18 April 1997).

---

[9] Dr. Friedman had proved that stress has profound physical consequences. (Reported in Science 1976). Today the once heretical notion that mental state can influence blood pressure is part of mainstream medical thinking, and Friedman is Benson's right-hand man at the Mind/Body Medical Institute (MBMI), a nonprofit research and education center they founded in Boston in 1988. Benson is a well-established researcher, with an endowed chair in his name at Harvard and a string of grant awards from the National Institutes of Health (NIH)-from the medical institutes, not from the Office of Alternative Medicine. "Benson is to be congratulated for opening the door to the links between mind and body," says former Surgeon General C. Everett Koop. "Good doctors have always used anything available to them in the healing of their patients." In his 1996 book Timeless Healing: The Power and Biology of Belief, Benson contends that humans are "wired for God"-that believing in God can improve your health. The calm instilled by faith itself can be a powerful force for healing.

A review of studies examining the effect of religion on healing in the *Archives of Family Medicine* revealed that people who practice religion have lower depression and suicide rates. They also seem to be able to deal better, both mentally and physically, with illness and recover from it faster than those who are not religiously committed. Perhaps one of the most intriguing findings is that devout people tend to have a lower incidence of high blood pressure.

A study funded by the National Institute of Health looked at the relationship between religion and blood pressure over a period of six years in more than 2,000 older adults. The investigators found that those who attended religious services at least once a day were 40% less likely to have high blood pressure than those who did so less frequently. And it doesn't appear that this correlation can be credited to a lifestyle that limits or rejects cigarettes and alcohol. The effect persisted even after adjusting for a variety of such factors, including smoking, and was particularly strong among those aged 65 to 74.

There are several hypotheses on how religion influences health. One is that religion helps people cope with stress. During any stressful situation the body's adrenal glands release a flood of chemicals that effectively raise heart rate and blood pressure. Praying or reading religious texts at home seems to help people maintain lower stress levels. The sense of social belonging and community that religion provides may also help minimize stress and its effects.

Religion appears to act as a buffer against mental and physical pain. In fact, 40% of 542 hospitalized adults reported that their religious faith was the most important factor in coping with their illness. And the results of a study published recently in the Journal of Psychiatry support this finding. Among elderly women recovering from hip fracture surgery, those with stronger religious beliefs and practices were less depressed and could walk greater distances when they left the hospital than those who were not so religious. While no direct causal relationship can be made from any of these studies, they certainly do reveal a link between religion and health.[10]

A few years ago, just three medical schools in the United States taught courses on religious issues in patient care. Today that number has increased tenfold.

A recent Newsweek survey found that 87% of adults believe God sometimes answers their prayers. A Nature poll found that 40% of all biologists, physicists, and mathematicians believe in a God who answers prayers.

Sadly we do not appreciate and thank God enough for his plethora of kindness. There are many little things that we take for granted in our lives. These include the ability for the body to repair itself in certain situations, or the marvelous ability to reproduce another life. God's creatures can reproduce themselves, a feat that with all human ingenuity available at the moment cannot be performed by any man-made creation. We are unable to produce an object that can reproduce itself. Truly we have to stand in awe as did Job (19:26) when he said the words "From my flesh I will see God."

Evolution or Creation

There is some confusion regarding evolution and creation, the primary element being that these topics address two different issues:

Creation deals with where everything came from and the primary cause for this to happen. Judaism has very clear answers on this subject. Our universe was created out of nothing by a Supreme Being who is infinite, all-powerful and all-knowing, above time

---

[10] The John Hopkins Medical Letter, November 1998.

and not affected by it. The Jewish name[11] for God symbolizes that He is above time and therefore has no beginning or end.

Evolution does not deal with the origins of the universe as that would posit creation and point to a Creator. It only theorizes the mechanism by which the universe changes over time. Atheists must believe that there was no creation from nothing and the physical universe that is presently in existence has always existed, albeit in a different form which evolved over time.

One of the more complex questions that exist on this idea that the universe has always been in existence is that we all know that matter is constantly being transformed into light and heat by the trillions and trillions of stars that exist. After billions and billions of years there should be a shortage of matter in the universe and there isn't. Why not?

There are major questions on evolutionist theory, chief of these being the lack of fossil evidence that evolution took place. Where are the fossils showing part-ape and part-human characteristics?[12] In fact, more than one hundred years of intense collecting by well-funded professional expeditions has not yet yielded any of the remains that Darwin had envisaged. Africa and the Middle East, the areas 'most likely' to have these remains have now been thoroughly searched. There are early ape-like remains and early hominid remains. The store of primate fossils has been multiplied a thousand fold since Darwin. The only 'missing link' so far discovered is the bogus Piltdown man, where a practical joker associated the jaw of an orangutan with the skull of a human.

---

[11] The question of who created God is therefore moot. God has no beginning or end. One of the cardinal principles of Judaism for which many Jews over the ages made the supreme sacrifice and gave their lives is that God has no physical form. Thus Jews are prohibited from having icons or statues. This is the third of the 'Ten Commandments.' The only representation of God we are allowed is His name. His name is the only thing we envisage when we think of God and is our connection to Him.

[12] This is called the 'missing link.' For more information see the book Shattering the Myths of Darwinism; Milton, Richard (International Traditions, LTD) 1997.

Darwin also gloomily confessed in <u>The Origin of the Species</u> that:

> "The number of intermediate varieties which have formerly existed on earth must be truly enormous. Why then is not every geological formation and every stratum full of such intermediate links? Geology assuredly does not reveal any such finely graduated organic chain; and this, perhaps is the most obvious and gravest objection which can be urged against my theory."

There has been a dramatic shift in scientific theory today. Most scientists who think about such issues have come to the realization that the universe as we know it came into being in seconds and minutes, just as the Bible states. Some scientists also conclude that a supreme being was behind creation.

There is a beautiful story of an atheist who came to visit a Rabbi. He asked the Rabbi to prove to him that God exists. The Rabbi had a gorgeous painting on the wall behind him. He pointed to it and said "look at that painting behind me. How do you like it?"

The individual was struck by its beauty, "It's a masterpiece." he cried, "Who painted it?"

The Rabbi looked at him with a twinkle in his eye. "Well," he said "one day I was sitting at my desk. By accident I knocked over the ink bottle and that caused this painting to occur."

The individual was incredulous. "There is no way Rabbi," he retorted, "that such a gorgeous masterpiece could be produced by accident!"

The Rabbi smiled "Think carefully about what you have just said. If a single painting cannot be produced or evolve through an accident, then how can this tremendously complex and exquisite world just come about by itself?"

In the same vein, Yale University's Dr. Harold Horowitz calculated that the odds against the random evolution of life are 1 in 10,000,000,000. Consider also the statement from Nobel Prize winner, Sir Fred Hoyle:

> "No matter how large an environment one considers, life cannot have had a random beginning. Troops of monkeys thundering away at random on typewriters could not produce the words of Shakespeare, for the practical reason that the whole observable universe is not large enough to contain the necessary monkey hordes, the necessary typewriters, and certainly the waste paper baskets required for the deposition of wrong attempts. The same is true for living material."

The beauty of the Torah is its simplicity. It takes very complex subjects, like creation, and describes them in terms that a lay person or even a child can grasp. The downside of this simplicity is that people take the Bible at face value as a very childish account, not realizing how deep it is.

At first, the scientific world believed that the universe was eternal. Today the accepted scientific theory for the creation of the universe is the 'Big Bang Theory.' According to this theory, the first stage of creation was a big bang started in a gargantuan black hole. The bible in its very second verse (Genesis 1:2), described this theory thousands of years before the scientists. 'And the land was waste and darkness was on the face of the deep.' Darkness on the face of the deep could be a euphemism for a black hole. The next verse describes the big bang as a great flash of light, the primeval light (or radiation) that predated the sun. I am sure that many people have read these verses many times without comprehending what could be their full import.[13]

13   This is not meant to be a definitive work on reconciling evolution and creationism but is meant to attract our attention to one of the mysteries on which we should focus. Many excellent works have been written in depth on this topic for example: (continued at right)

Not only does the Big Bang Theory support the idea of God's creation of the universe, it even resembles the chronology of Creation given in the Bible. Just as it is stated in *Genesis* that God created light before He created the sun and the stars, which seems enigmatic, the Big Bang Theory proposes that the sun and the stars came into being long after the initial explosion. They are merely 'latter-day' by-products of the original radiation (light) which appeared out of nothing.

Discussing the Big Bang Theory, and why scientists were irritated by it, Dr. Robert Jastrow, director of NASA's Goddard Institute for Space Studies, had this to say:

> "I think that part of the answer is that scientists cannot bear the thought of a natural phenomenon that cannot be explained, even with unlimited time and money. There is a kind of religion in science…This religious faith of the scientist is violated by the discovery that the world had a beginning under the conditions in which the known laws of physics are not valid, and as a product of forces or circumstances we cannot discover. When that happens the scientist has lost control. If he really examined the implications, he would be traumatized. As usual, when faced with trauma, the mind reacts by ignoring the implications. The main problem though, was that the Big Bang Theory pointed to God, tending to confirm the account of Creation in the Bible."

In 1978, Dr. Jastrow published an article in the New York Times Magazine. This outlined the evidence that our universe inexplicably burst into existence. It concluded:

Bereshit and the Big Bang by Gerald Schroeder (Bantam 1990); The Obvious Proof by Gershon Robinson and Mordechai Steinman (CIS 1993); In The Beginning: Biblical Creation & Science by Nathan Aviezer (Ktav 1990); Challenge by Aryeh Carmell & Cyril Domb (Feldheim 1978); God and the Astronomers by Robert Jastrow (W.W. Norton 1978).

"This is an exceedingly strange development, unexpected by all but the theologians. They have always accepted the word of the Bible: 'In the beginning God created heaven and earth.'[14] For the scientist who has lived by his faith in the power of reason, the story ends like a bad dream. He has scaled the mountains of ignorance; he is about to conquer the highest peak; as he pulls himself over the final rock, he is greeted by a band of theologians who have been sitting there for centuries."

Even with the widespread acceptance of the big bang theory many questions still remain, the major ones being the discrepancy of billions of years that the bible glosses over, and the creation of Adam and Eve, which according to Jewish tradition, took place nearly six thousand years ago. It is very interesting to note that all social scientists agree that historic man dates back around ten thousand or so years in the same order of time that our tradition asserts the creation of Adam and Eve, not the millions of years that were previously mentioned.

What happened in the billions of years since the creation of the universe until the creation of man? What about fossils dated to be millions of years old, where are they from?

There are many possible answers to these questions, among them the following five:

1. There was an instantaneous creation of galaxies and fossils and, just as the first tree was created fully-formed and the first

---

[14] A famous entertainer has a wonderful routine. He said that when God created the earth, the Bible records his reaction as "He saw it was very good." This was an inclusive statement covering all the various creations up till then. It is as if God when He created the rabbit said it is "very good." When God created a tree He said modestly "Very good." Compare the creations of human beings to those of God. When a car company builds a car they declare: "It's fantastic! It's revolutionary!" When an appliance company makes a refrigerator, they say "Spectacular! Unprecedented!" The refrigerator breaks down. The car doesn't work. The rabbit is still hopping. The tree is still blossoming.

man was created fully-grown, so too the earth was created, complete and fully-aged.

2. The scientific deductions regarding the age of the world are based on extrapolation of data taken only within the last hundred or so years. Extrapolation becomes increasingly inaccurate over long time periods.

3. From the time God created the universe, it evolved under the laws of nature to produce stars, planets, the sun and moon, and genetic material (the seeds or potential for vegetation). This took many billions of years if the time was measured locally, but from the Torah's viewpoint (cosmic time, time within an intense gravitational field) it only took several twenty-four hour days. Even though the laws of nature were observed, the evolution was not accidental. It followed from the initial conditions God had established at the moment of creation.

4. The fossil record and the early universe indicate the previous worlds that, according to Kabbalah, were created and destroyed before this one. (This is the viewpoint of the Tiferet Yisrael in his commentary to the Mishnah Masechet Sanhedrin)

5. Fossils and other apparent manifestations of earlier times were actually formed only a few thousand years ago, either by processes we do not understand yet, or by physical laws that have since changed.[15]

---

[15] Ernst Chain (1906-1979) and two others were awarded the 1945 **Nobel Prize for Physiology or Medicine. Chain identified the structure of penicillin**, and isolated the active substance. He is considered to be one of the founders of the field of antibiotics. Concerning Darwin's theory of evolution, Chain found it to be "a very feeble attempt" to explain the origin of species based on assumptions so flimsy that "it can hardly be called a theory." He saw the reliance on chance mutations as a "hypothesis based on no evidence and irreconcilable with the facts." He wrote: "These classic evolutionary theories are a gross oversimplification of an immensely complex and intricate mass of facts, and it amazes me that they were swallowed so uncritically and readily, and for such a long time, by so many scientists without a murmur of protest." Chain concluded that he "would rather believe in fairies than in such wild speculation" as Darwinism.

The Importance of the Present

There are a lot of mysteries in the past on which the Torah (both written and oral) sheds light. However, we should not overly focus on mystery. This is hinted to in the first letter of the Torah, which is a 'bet' 'בּ' Enclosed on three sides, it advises us that we are limited in our understanding of what is above, below and what came before us.

For those who have come to believe in an all-knowing, all-powerful, invisible, one God who created the universe, there is less mystery. The traditional Jewish conviction has always been not to worry where the world came from, but where it is now and the direction in which it is heading. We have to concern ourselves with matters that we can change and alter, the present and future, not the past. The future of our existence, and that of our progeny, is to a great extent in our hands. Moses, our greatest prophet said with immense wisdom: "The hidden things belong to God, whereas the revealed matters are in our hands."[16] Judaism is a very practical religion, concerned with the things we can do, and not those that are beyond our reach.

Paraphrasing Moses: "This mitzvah I am commanding you is not too wondrous or too far away. It is not in heaven, that you should say who will go up to the heavens and take it for us and teach it to us and we will do it. It is not across the sea that you should say who will cross the sea and take it for us and teach us and we will do it. The matter is very close to you in your mouths and in your hearts to do it." (Deuteronomy 30:11).

Whereas other religions focus on death and the mystery surrounding it, Judaism focuses on life. Although the Prophets and the Talmud are replete with mention of life after death and the messianic era, in the five books of Moses there is no explicit mention of it. The

---

[16] Deuteronomy 29:28.

Bible does not focus our attention on mysteries, but on the present in a very practical way.

Approaching God through the Torah, - History

It is important to learn history for the lessons contained within it, not just history for its own sake. "Remember the days of old, understand the years of generation after generation. Ask your father and he will relate to you, your elders and they will tell you."[17]

The first Rashi[18] on the Bible seems to disagree by asking why we need the first book of the Torah, Genesis (Bereshit). His question and answer implies that the Torah is not a history book but a moral and ethical work that reveals God's will to us.

There is a famous debate between Rashi and Ramban[19] as to whether or not the historical details of the Torah are in chronological order. Rashi takes the view that the message is more important than the form. According to him[20] the chronological order is not as important as the message the Torah is relating. Sometimes the Torah puts certain incidents together to emphasize a message, not because the two incidents are chronologically in order.[21] In contrast, Ramban holds to a literal view. He insists that the Torah is both a historically valid document that is chronologically accurate, and a moral code.[22]

What they both agree on is that the Torah is a moral and ethical

[17] Deuteronomy 32:7.
[18] Rabbi Shlomo Yitzhaki the eleventh century French Biblical commentator, see glossary at the end of the book.
[19] Rabbi Moses Ben Nachman, famous Torah commentator and Talmudist, see glossary at the end of the book.
[20] See Rashi on Bereshit 6:3 and many other places.
[21] Hence, Rashi on Bereshit 39:1 gives two reasons, other than chronology, why the account of Joseph being sold into Egypt is interrupted by the account of what transpired between Judah and Tamar.
[22] The exception to this rule is made by the Ramban on the beginning of Parashat Acharei-Mot.

Divinely-inspired code for living life to the fullest potential. The history of the past is important if it helps us to live more moral, ethical and fulfilling lives.

The Torah is a moral guide that teaches us how real men and women grappled with life's difficulties, and how God wants us to act. The goal of the Torah is not to teach us history for the sake of cold scholarly research into past civilizations, but to grant us insight into how to conduct our lives and deal with the problems and issues that we face daily.

A person who has delved deeply into Torah cannot help but be amazed at its tremendous insights into human psychology and behavior. The beauty of how the Torah system meshes within itself and with the world is truly amazing and points to its Divine origins.

Mysteries of the Future

The mysteries of the past cannot be compared to the mysteries of the future. At least we have some points of reference regarding the past but not the future, apart from the predictions made in the Torah and by the prophets. We don't even know what the next few minutes will bring.

Rabbi Moshe Haim Luzatto,[23] in his important work The Path of the Just, compares this world to a maze. In the Middle Ages, the kings and queens of Europe had lots of leisure time on their hands.

---

[23] 1707-1746. Born in Padua, Italy into a distinguished family, his genius was obvious at an early age. Besides his complete mastery of the entire Biblical, Rabbinic and Kabbalistic literature, he was thoroughly educated in the science and literature of that time. In 1740, at the age of 33, he published the Mesilat Yesharim (Path of the Just). It is a moving, inspiring work describing how a thoughtful Jew may climb the ladder of purification until he attains the level of holiness. In 1743 Rabbi Moshe Haim left for Israel with his family, unfortunately, just a few short years later, he and his family perished in a plague. In one of the standard texts of Modern Hebrew literature, Rabbi Moshe Haim is referred to as the father of modern Jewish literature.

To pass the time they invented many unique games. Outside Hampton Court in England and the Palace of Versailles in France are hedges planted in the shape of mazes. The royal family would have garden parties during which they would blindfold their guests and lead them into the center of the maze. They derived great pleasure from watching them from a balcony above try to find their way out. What can we learn from this?

Imagine that God placed us in such a maze, the maze of life. The decisions we continuously make in the course of our lives are like making turns in this maze. We cannot see where the path we are on will lead us. A wrong turn can have eternal repercussions. And yet God allows us to turn where we choose, to exercise our own free will.

With all our wisdom and knowledge we don't have a clue as to what the next few minutes have in store for us, much less predicting events of the next week or year. The future is dark, yet there are lights that illuminate and direct the pathways of our lives. King Solomon in Proverbs 6:23 made a remarkable statement: "A Mitzvah is a candle and the Torah is a light". This means that following the instructions of God gives us direction in life.

Notes

_____

_____

_____

_____

_____

_____

_____

_____

_____

_____

_____

_____

_____

_____

_____

_____

Chapter 2. Purpose

Introduction

The vast majority of Jewish youth have been brought up estranged from a vibrant, spiritual Judaism. In North America, they have been brought up to view Judaism as 'a bagels and lox religion.' At best Judaism is viewed as a 'social' phenomenon, with quaint customs, a different diet, and lots of fundraising. At worst it is viewed as being totally incomprehensible, out of touch with the realities of modern day existence.

The reactions of our youth today are twofold: a) They lose themselves in the vanities of this world. b) They are so desperate for spirituality that cults and other 'religions' ensnare them.

a) Lost in Vanity, - The Trap of Materialism

In Pirke Avot (4:16), our sages of blessed memory compare this world to a corridor before the palace. That is, this world is not permanent. It is just a temporary passageway to the next world.

We easily and frequently forget that this world is not everlasting, and we get caught up in the struggle for materialism that abounds around us.

On the one hand there is no mitzvah to be poor or to live in miserable circumstances. Riches are never scoffed at in the Torah. On the contrary, wealth is viewed as a blessing from God. The idea that wealth is a blessing is fundamental to Judaism. It is mentioned in the second paragraph of the Shema (Deuteronomy 11).

Maimonides (Laws of Teshuvah 9:1) further explains this idea:

"The blessing of wealth is not an end in itself, but a means that should be used for the performance of more good deeds. Fortunate are the people who view their material possessions as the instruments to perfect themselves and the world."

On the other hand, wealth can be a test. We may build large houses and buy expensive furniture. Understandably, we want to live well, but we have to realize that we are just temporary and cannot take these things with us. This was the mistake made by the Pharaohs of Egypt. Their wealth was buried with them in magnificent burial chambers in enormous pyramids that are among the wonders of the ancient world. These massive mausoleums were built utilizing slave labor at great cost, both in terms of human lives lost in the construction, and in the financial expenses involved.

The Pharaohs thought that they needed all their wealth and belongings for their long voyage to the next world. We now know for sure that they were terribly mistaken. Obviously they could not take anything with them. Ironically, the vast majority of their great fortune was stolen by grave robbers. The rest, including their beautifully-preserved remains, ended up in important museums around the world. King Solomon summed up the physical prowess of even the greatest human beings in a few words; "Vanity of vanities, all is vanity." Kohelet 1:1.

There is a beautiful story of an American Jew who was touring through pre-Second World War Europe. He had heard a lot about the Hafetz Haim, and so on his way through Poland he decided to go and visit this famous Rabbi. Expecting the great Rabbi to be living a lifestyle in accordance with his fame, the tourist was taken aback when the door to the very humble dwelling of the great Rabbi was answered by the Hafetz Haim himself. He was overawed by the great leader's simple demeanor and by his humble diminutive presence. When the wonder started to wear off, he started to look around the Rabbi's dwelling. The first thing that struck him about it was the paucity of furniture. He was amazed and could not hold himself back from asking this question in great wonderment "Rabbi, where is your furniture?"

"Where is yours?" was the quick response.

"I'm just passing through here, Rabbi." answered the tourist.

"So am I." answered the Hafetz Haim with a small smile.

We forget this most important fact:

We are all tourists passing through this world, which is only a temporary state of being for us. Let us not make it the focus of all our energies.

b) Ensnared By Spiritual Falsehoods

In their search for spirituality and meaning, many of our young people have joined various cults, the majority of whose members in the United States happen to be Jews. They are unaware of the inner satisfaction and sense of purpose and mission that vibrant Judaism can give a person. They are searching in strange places and are being misled in droves by charlatans who play on their naïveté and their spiritual thirst.

There are two beautiful stories that illustrate this point:

A poor Jewish peasant had a dream that there was a pot of gold buried near a local bridge. Full of hope, he went to the bridge. A watchman was guarding the bridge. He observed the Jew circling around the area of the bridge as if he was looking for something. "Hey!" he shouted, "What are you looking for?" The poor Jew came closer and sheepishly explained his dream, his desperate situation, and his hopes of finding the gold. The watchman was a jovial fellow. He burst out laughing. "Don't believe these silly dreams. Why, I myself had a similar dream last night. I dreamed that a poor Jewish peasant in a nearby town had a pot of gold buried under his fireplace. I am not going crazy worrying about these insane dreams."

The peasant listened to the watchman's dream with bated breath. He had just described his own house. He rushed home and dug under his fireplace. Sure enough, he found a pot of gold and became very wealthy.

The moral of this story is that many people are looking for spiritual satisfaction in distant, exotic lands and in strange religions that their forefathers never knew, but they are unaware of the treasures of their own religion and heritage.

The second story is about an elderly Jewish woman who joined an Indian cult in her neighborhood. The members of the cult were taken aback by the combination of her very Jewish appearance and her age. They questioned her about her seriousness and her realization of what was entailed in her joining. The woman attended all meetings religiously for six months. The cult planned a trip to India to visit the 'holy' man, who was the leader of the cult. Everyone was amazed to see that the old lady was the first one to sign up for this trip.

The group arrived in India and was taken to the massive temple of the 'holy' man. There were two lines of people waiting for admission to the holy man, one long and one short. The woman inquired as to the significance of these two lines.

"Well," she was told, "The long line is for those who want to discuss matters at length with the 'holy' man. The short line is for those who are limited to saying four words."

The old woman went and stood in the short line. When her turn came for an audience, she shocked all the onlookers, and the 'holy' man was visibly moved. "Moishele!" she cried bitterly, "Please come home."

This anecdote illustrates the sorry state of Jewry today. We have lost tens of thousands of our spiritually-sensitive, searching young people to strange meaningless gods because we have not explained and reiterated enough the purpose, rationale and spirituality inherent in Judaism.

Purpose

a) Individual Perfection

The first part of our mission is on the micro-scale: to perfect ourselves as individuals, spiritually and ethically, so as to emulate and draw close to our Creator and give good examples to the rest of humanity. By doing this we will also earn our portion in the world to come.

The basic components of society are individuals. If each individual is striving for moral, ethical, and spiritual perfection, then society as a whole will be enriched and elevated. But if, as is presently the case, imperfect societies are blamed for the most part, not on evil individuals, but on bad government, individuals will never strive for perfection and society will never realize this goal.

This, the perfection of each individual, is the secret of a perfect society. Ignoring this is one of the biggest mistakes made by present-day social architects. The brilliance of the Torah system is that it starts from the ground up. We are all responsible for our own individual perfection. Worldwide perfection will only come about if all individuals are perfect.

There is a famous Midrash which highlights the idea that individual perfection is one of the main goals of God's Torah. The Midrash Tanchuma Shemini 7 quotes Rabbi Judah the Prince[24] as asking rhetorically: "What does God care if the Jews eat without shechitah (ritual slaughter)?" He answered by expounding on a verse from Psalms 18 "The sayings of God purify. The mitzvot (commandments) were given to us to test and discipline each one of us, in order to purify us and make us better human beings."

The Sefer Hahinuch[25] (The Book of Education) in Mitzvah 16 gives us a perspective on the rationale of the mitzvot:

> "Know that a person is formed according to his deeds. His heart and all his thoughts inevitably follow the path set by the activities in which he engages, whether for good or for bad. Even a consummate villain whose heart is filled with evil, and whose thoughts turn to nothing except evil, would find himself instantly drawn to good if he were to expend his energy and efforts constantly on Torah and Mitzvot, even if his motives were neither pure nor heavenly. For this reason, God chose to give us many mitzvot so that they could engage our thoughts and be the focus of our activities. Through these goodly deeds, we should become good and merit everlasting life."

---

[24] First and second century CE sage and editor of the Mishnah.

[25] Sefer Hahinukh, an excellent and indispensable addition to any library of Judaica, was written toward the latter half of the thirteenth century. The Hinuch contains a discussion of the 613 mitzvot organized according to the order of the weekly Torah portion. Based primarily on the Rambam and Ramban, each mitzvah is divided into four parts: a) A brief statement of the essence of the mitzvah. b) The reason for the mitzvah. This is probably the most original part of the work. c) A summary of the details of the mitzvah, and d) when and to whom the mitzvah applies.   This book was written for the youth of the time, to be read by them on the Sabbath and on holidays. It emphasizes throughout that a person's inner being is shaped by the actions he performs. Thus, proper performance of mitzvot influences the doer to become a better person.

Sefer Hahinukh is written in a simple, clear and inspiring style. There have been several proposals put forward as to the identity of the author, but until today his anonymity is preserved and this has not affected its universal appeal and continued popularity.

There is a relatively new branch of psychology entitled behavior modification that posits that our thoughts follow our deeds, and that it is possible to change the way a person thinks by first modifying his or her behavior. This seems to be the reason for the commandments advanced by the above.

The Vilna Gaon,[26] in a small but immensely powerful volume entitled Even Shelema, states that the main function for a person in this world is to perfect his or her character traits. A person who learns the whole Torah, with all the intellectual stimulation involved and theoretical knowledge obtained, but does not perfect his or her character, has not achieved this goal.

Rabbi Moshe Haim Luzatto, in his book The Path of the Just, discusses the topic of individual perfection in great detail. In his introduction he laments the fact that so few people, even from the so-called 'religious' element, focus themselves on this ideal of serving God and perfecting this service.

> "There are many intelligent people who spend their time on their professions as lawyers, doctors, accountants, astronomers, scientists, and mathematicians. Others spend their time learning Torah: Talmud, Mishnah, Halachah, and Midrash. But few devote their thought and study to the perfection of serving God. They think it is so obvious they are doing so, that it does not require thought. Frequently, the idea of perfecting one's service of God has been left to those of limited intelligence, so that when one sees someone engaged in saintly conduct, one cannot help but suspect them of lacking intelligence. The wise lack perfection because they don't spend enough time pondering it. Those of less intelligence lack perfection because of their limited ability to grasp

---

[26] Rabbi Elijah of Vilna, sixteenth century child prodigy and leader of Lithuanian Jewry.

concepts. The result is people think that perfection is achieved through reading the book of Psalms all day, or engaging in fasting and other kinds of self mortification. The truth is that saintliness is far from that concept.

King Solomon in Proverbs 2:4 states: "If you will seek it as silver and search for it as a treasure, then you will understand the fear of God."

You know how much time, effort and money the oil companies expend in looking for oil, and how much time, energy and money the mining companies spend looking for precious natural resources. This is how much we should be spending on trying to achieve individual perfection.

b) To be Ethical and Moral Role Models for the Whole World

The second purpose of Judaism is explicit in the Torah[27] and is an idea with which we end our thrice-daily prayers: 'To perfect the world under the kingship of God.' Our mission is to create an ethical, moral, monotheistic world civilization where there will be no hunger, poverty, lawlessness, or strife; a society in which people will be engaged in brotherhood and peace, and devote the greater part of their time to the pursuit of knowledge of God.

We talk about ourselves as being the children of Abraham and Sarah, whom we look up to as our ancestors, as opposed to the other nations of the world who are called the children of Noah. One of the aspects of being an ancestor is that of being a role model for progeny. Abraham and Sarah are the role models for us to emulate and not Noah, even though we are also descended from Noah.

---

[27] Exodus 19:6.

Among many misconceptions that people have about Judaism is that Abraham was the first Jew.[28] He wasn't. Judaism as we know it did not exist before the Torah was given at Sinai, and hence there were no Jews befor the giving of the Torah.[29]

Abraham and Noah were both on very high spiritual levels. They both communicated with God, but we have no record that Noah tried to reach out to others, or that he tried to improve society. When God told him that He was going to destroy the world and instructed him to build a boat for himself and his family, Noah's response was silence. He didn't plead with God to save the world. He didn't try and change people's attitudes. He minded his own business and built the ark. When people would come to him and ask him questions, he would answer them, but he wouldn't go out of his way to reach out to others.

Let us contrast this with Abraham's behavior. Abraham truly cared about other human beings. When God told Abraham that He was planning to destroy the city of Sodom and its environs, Abraham argued back spiritedly in defense of these people, even though the vast majority of them were evil.

Abraham also tried to change society by spreading his belief in an invisible, all-powerful, infinite Creator and Ruler of the Universe. The Torah hints at this in Genesis 12:5, when it mentions that Abraham and Sarah moved to Canaan with all the souls that they had made in Haran. Rashi explains that these 'souls' were people

[28] The name Jew is a derivative of the name Judah, one of the sons of Jacob, after whom one of the twelve tribes was named. After the exile and dispersion of the ten 'lost' tribes by the Assyrians in approximately 700 BCE, the vast majority of the people who survived were from the tribe of Judah, hence they became known as Jews. Mordechai in the story of Purim (Megillat Esther) was one of the first to be called a Jew (Yehudi).

[29] Ramban (Exodus 25:2) learns the laws of conversion from the events at Sinai at which the Israelites formally converted to Judaism. Just as the male Israelites were circumcised, so too male converts must be circumcised. Just as the Israelites went through the stream by Mt. Sinai, so too a convert must immerse into a ritual pool of water, and just as the Israelites accepted the Torah at Sinai, so too a convert must accept the Torah as the standard for his or her lifestyle.

whom they had persuaded to accept an ethical, monotheistic way of life.

This is the second part of our mission, on a macro level, to be ethical and moral human beings and upright members of society who will be good role models for the rest of society, and will change society through osmosis, either by their interaction with others or just by spreading the lessons of the Bible. The Torah stresses (Exodus 19:6) that we are to be a kingdom of priests and a holy nation, priests to whom? The answer is that we have to be role models like our forefather Abraham, and to help make this world more ethical, moral and spiritual.

Most people have a general idea of how the Jews originated how they won their land and established their kingdoms. However, most people do not realize the influence which the Torah, Moses the lawgiver, our poets, writers and religious teachers - the men and women known as the prophets have had on the world. Their words have resounded through the centuries and their thoughts affect our lives today.

The Bible has influenced the mind and happiness of the Western world more than any battle ever fought, any invention ever made, or any idea ever expressed. It has inspired the religion, the language, the arts, the conduct, the fears and the hopes of almost every nation on earth. Over the last sixty or so years, one of the most consistently prominent issues on the world stage has been Israel and Jews. Many nations, more populous and with much greater land mass, have hardly been heard about. However, Jews are news. God's plan is to keep us at center stage. Judaism is by far the smallest[30] of the major world religions and is the mother religion of both Christianity and Islam. It is considered a major

---

[30] The World Factbook gives the population as 7,095,217,980 (July 2013 est.) and the distribution of religions as Christian 31.50% Muslim 22.74%, Hindu 13.8%, Buddhist 6.77%, Sikh 0.35%, Jewish 0.22%, Baha'i 0.11%, other religions 10.95%, non-religious 9.66%, atheists 2.01% (2010 est.)

world religion not because of the number of its adherents, but because of its impact on world morality and ethics. Ironically, the biggest enemies of the Jewish people have been the ones who recognized the power of the message of Judaism.

The test of a people's greatness is not the number of its citizens, nor the size of its cities, nor the wealth of its millionaires. The real test lies in a people's effort to improve the mind, the character and the well-being of humanity, to give life new directions, and to extend justice in human society. This is why the small Jewish people are of such interest and importance to the world.

The prophecies of the future by Isaiah the prophet are well-known, so well-known that the United Nations headquarters in New York has an Isaiah wall. In Chapter 2, Verses 2-4, Isaiah gives a universal message of hope and purpose:

> "It will happen in the end of days: The Mountain of the Temple of Hashem will be firmly established as the head of the mountains, and it will be exalted above the hills, and all the nations will stream to it. Many people will go and say, 'Come let us go up to the mountain of Hashem, to the Temple of the God of Jacob, and He will teach us of His ways and we will walk in His paths.' For from Zion will the Torah come forth, and the word of Hashem from Jerusalem. He will judge among the nations, and will settle the arguments of many peoples. They shall beat their swords into plows and their spears into pruning hooks; nation will not lift sword against nation and they will no longer study warfare."

Again in Chapter 11 he predicts, in parable form, that there will be universal peace and brotherhood.

"A staff will emerge from the stump of Jesse and a shoot will sprout from his roots. The spirit of Hashem will sprout from his roots. The spirit of Hashem will rest upon him, a spirit of wisdom and understanding, a spirit of knowledge and fear of God. He will be imbued with a spirit of fear for Hashem, and will not need to judge by what his eyes see nor decide by what his ears hear. He will judge the destitute with righteousness, and decide with fairness for the humble of the earth. He will strike the wicked of the world with the rod of his mouth, and with the breath of his lips he will slay the wicked. Righteousness will be the girdle round his loins.

The wolf will live with the sheep and the leopard will lie down with the kid; and a calf, a lion's whelp...will walk together...They will neither injure nor destroy in all of my sacred mountain; for the earth will be as full of knowledge of God as water covering the sea bed."

Judaism is broad and universal. This is the reason the Rabbis[31] point out that the Torah was given in the wilderness. It was given in a no-man's land, a place open to everyone, all persons, of all races, so that people should not say that the nations of the world have no portion in the Torah.

However, when it comes to where Jews should live, the Torah is very specific. Why do we have to live in a specific location?[32] This is an idea unique to Judaism that is not found in any other religion. The reason, I think, is that:

God wants the Jewish nation on its own land, in its own state to build a perfect, moral, ethical society that will serve as a

---

[31] Mechilta D'Rabi Yishmael, Yitro Parashah 1.
[32] Bereshit 12:1.

role model for the rest of the world, a society to be based on the triple foundations of monotheism, righteousness and justice.

This was the case in the heyday of the Jewish commonwealth in the days of King Solomon.

How to Spread Ethical Monotheism in the World

Kind David, toward the end of his life, had a desire to build a dwelling place for God's Ark. (Samuel 2:7, 13) The Bible tells us that he was not allowed to do so. The reason usually given is that his hands were full of blood. He was constantly engaged in warfare to protect his kingdom and people.

The second reason given is implicit in the verses. He built himself a lavish palace and only then expressed concern that there was no permanent dwelling for the Ark. His priorities were skewed and should have been reversed.

The third reason is a rational one that has been advanced from a social perspective. His kingdom was not sufficiently established from a social and economic perspective to undertake the massive spiritual project of building a house of God. These three reasons represent different ideas.

Let us assume that the building of a house for God symbolizes spreading the word of God in the world.

a) This cannot be achieved in a violent manner. A person whose hands are full of blood cannot build the house of God. A similar idea is also mentioned by the Torah at the end of Parashat Yitro (Exodus 20:22) after the 'Ten Commandments' are mentioned. [33]

---

[33] In a recent survey reported by the Maariv Newspaper in Israel, the following startling statistics were reported: 88% of the adult population of Israel does not remember all of the Ten Commandments. 25% had difficulty recalling even one. 40% do not know what the Five Books of Moses are. (continued bottom of next page)

Three more commandments were given to Moses on Sinai that are not as well-known and hardly ever mentioned, which govern Temple worship. One of them is the following:

> "And if you will make the altar out of stone, do not build it from hewn stone, because you have swung your sword over it and desecrated it."

God does not want his altar to be built from stones that were cut by implements made from the same materials as those used in implements of war and killing.

If these are the figures for Israel, I dread to think what the figures for the Diaspora would be. On Shabbat Yitro, and again on the Festival of Shavuot, the 'Ten Commandments' are read in synagogues around the world. Unfortunately, many people have only heard of the 'Ten Commandments' because of the movie. It's probably a good idea to refresh our memories and look at the original script.

To clarify a misconception, nowhere does the Torah mention 'Ten Commandments.' Rather, the term 'Aseret Hadevarim' is used (Exodus 34:28 and Deuteronomy 4:13; 10:4) which means the 'Ten Sayings.' According to the great scholar Rambam, these 'Ten Sayings' include fourteen commandments as follows:

1. To believe in the existence of one, indivisible, all powerful, invisible, unchanging God.
2. Not to believe in any other god besides Him.
3. Not to make any shapes or forms that are worshipped.
4. Not to bow to any idolatry.
5. Not to serve any idolatry in its normal way of service.
6. Not to take an oath containing God's name falsely.
7. To sanctify the Sabbath with words. (Kiddush).
8. Not to perform creative forms of work on the Sabbath.
9. To honor one's parents.
10. Not to shed innocent blood.
11. Not to commit adultery.
12. Not to kidnap.
13. Not to bear false witness.
14. Not to covet neighbor's property, wife or husband, or belongings and plan to obtain them for oneself.

Another widespread misconception is that these are the only 10 commandments. There are many more commandments in the Torah (Five Books of Moses 613 commandments (mitzvot) in total. They cover the whole gamut of human and spiritual relationships. Of these, 248 are positive dos, and 365 are negative don'ts. There are over twice as many negative commandments as there are positive ones that are applicable to us on a daily basis. Most of us fulfill them anyway by default. For instance, just by not stealing, committing adultery, or murder we fulfill negative commandments.

Violence has no part or role in the spreading of God's word in the world. God's word has to be spread through conviction and role-play.

Rabbi Samson Raphael Hirsch, in his commentary on the Bible, puts this concept very eloquently:

> "Not destruction, not sacrifice, nor giving up life, is the meaning and purpose of the altar...right and humanity must build the altar, and the realms of right and humanness, not the mastery of the sword, is to spread from it. In the 'Hall of Stone' adjoining the altar of stone, the Supreme Court (Sanhedrin) was housed...the altar is the symbol of Jewish Justice."

Contrast this idea with the mass conversions under threat of death, that were carried out in the name of religion by two major religions in previous years and today by ISIL in the name of Islam.

b) The second idea, that David built his lavish palace before he thought about a dwelling for God, represents the importance of priorities in life. David would have been excused, had he built himself the simplest dwelling fit for a king. But he went overboard materialistically and was thus not worthy of building a spiritual dwelling. This teaches us that even though a certain amount of materialism is necessary for our physical well-being we must not lose sight of our spiritual goals and drown in a sea of physicality. The Mishnah (Avot 3:17) sums up this idea with its dictum "If there is no flour, there can be no Torah study, and if there is no Torah study, there can be no flour." Flour represents physical and material wealth. This must go hand in hand with the spiritual endeavors of man.

c) The third reason advanced was the fact that the Kingdom of Israel at that time was not sufficiently stable from an economic and social perspective for such a massive spiritual undertaking. It was constantly in a state of war.

On an individual level, a person cannot attain a high level of spirituality unless he or she is physically healthy, mentally stable and wise, and economically sound. These three things must be attained before high spiritual aspirations can be reached.

The Talmud[34] quotes Rabbi Yochanan as saying that God only rests his spirit on a person who possesses the following: wisdom, physical might, and financial wealth. Rambam, the great Rabbi, doctor and philosopher, discussed this concept in the Laws of Prophecy.[35] He describes a lower level of prophecy as requiring the following traits: Wisdom, total control over desires, and an extremely broad intellect. **A prophet is a person who sanctifies himself or herself to be in tune with the spiritual world.**

This connects to our forefather Jacob's dream (Bereshit 28:12): Jacob was on his way to his uncle Lavan's house. While camping out in the fields one night, he saw a vision of a ladder, with its base resting firmly on the ground and its head in the heavens, angels were climbing up and down the ladder.
There are many interpretation of the symbolism of this dream:

1. The angels are spiritual entities that accompanied Jacob to protect him on his travels. Rashi explains that there are different angels for different areas of the world i.e. different states of Divine providence depending on where one lives. When a person leaves a certain place their spiritual auras also change some for the better and some for the worse.

2. The ladder represents the timeline of Jewish history. The angels climbing up and down the ladder represent the nations

---

[34] Nedarim 35.
[35] Yesodei Hatorah 7:1, see Kessef Mishnah.

who will become great and ultimately fade away. God was on top of the ladder as He ultimately watches over human history.

3. This ladder also represents human beings. We are a synthesis of the material and the physical worlds. Our feet must rest firmly on the ground, we need to be practical.

Our physical existence is important and has to be provided for, but our visions and aspirations - the angels - should be directed upwards to God. We need to realize that we can go either up or down the spiritual escalator of life.

Sanctifying God's Name in Public / Kiddush Hashem

We can influence our surroundings most by being positive role models to those around us. This form of behavior has been traditionally called Kiddush Hashem (sanctifying God's name). The sanctification of God's name is achieved when an individual known to be a believer in God is familiar to everyone around for his or her meticulous adherence to God's law, both in the spiritual realm and in those laws that affect relations with his or her neighbors.

The Midrash[36] relates the story of Rabbi Shimon Ben Shetach, a famous leader of the Sanhedrin, the highest court in Israel, some two thousand years ago. The Rabbi sent students to acquire a donkey on his behalf. They bought one from a gentile. It came fully equipped with a saddle and bridle. On the way back from the market the students discovered a very precious stone hidden under the saddle. They rushed to the Rabbi with the good news. He was now an extremely wealthy man. The Rabbi's response was totally unexpected. "I purchased a donkey; I did not purchase a jewel. Return it to its rightful owner."

---

[36] Deuteronomy Rabbah 3.

The students hastened to do their teacher's bidding. The gentile former owner of the donkey was very grateful. "Praised is Rabbi Shimon Ben Shetach and praised is the God of the Jews." was his emotional response. Rabbi Shimon Ben Shetach's behavior was a sanctification of God's name and a good example for all of us to follow.

Distractions from Purpose, - The Human Rat Race

We are all busy, always on the go, trying to earn a living and achieve all the modern-day trappings of success. The rat race never ends. The Jew in worldly activity faces frequent challenges to his or her fidelity to Torah values and mitzvah observance. He or she may be struggling to make a mark on a particular field of endeavor, a goal which may appear to be threatened as a result of his or her adherence to Torah guidelines. The time and energy devoted to 'making it' also subtracts from time available for striving for perfection.[37]

A wealthy landowner once wanted to reward one of his loyal followers, whose name was Sam. The landowner told Sam to come to him the next day and he would give him as much land as Sam could run around in one day.

The following day, punctually at sunrise, an eager and excited Sam came to the landowner to begin his run, which he had to complete by sunset.

Sam started off at a good pace. On the way he passed his beloved wife. She tried to stop him to ask him to do an errand for her. "Later, later," he cried, barely pausing, "Can't you see that I am very busy right now?"

---

[37] The Torah also expounds on some business ethics which, if followed, can lead to success and a reputation as an ethical and trustworthy businessperson.

It was midday already. He had covered ground, but the pace was getting to him. "You know?" he said to himself, "If I run just a bit faster, I can cover more ground." He accelerated his pace.

"Dad!" he heard a small voice crying "Dad, can you help me with my homework?"
"No time, son, no time." the father muttered "Can't you see I'm busy?"

His son was crestfallen. "You always say that dad. You never have time for me."

Sam felt sorry for his son. "Poor boy, I'll make it up to you later. After all, I am doing this for you."

"Sam!" the Rabbi shouted with desperation in his voice. "Sam, can you please help us? We need one more man for the minyan."

"I'm sorry Rabbi." puffed Sam, running away, "I can't make it today. I'm real busy, but call me tomorrow. I can't promise, but I'll try."

Close to sunset, a small crowd had gathered around the landowner. Everyone was amazed. Sam had covered a tremendous amount of ground. He came into view, puffing and panting. Everyone cheered. "Sam," the landowner said, "congratulations! You have really achieved a great deal."

"Thanks," muttered Sam and then, clutching his chest he fell down and died of heart failure.

"Give him six feet." said the landowner.

This is a parable of our lives. We are always running around, trying to make ends meet. We don't have, or rather; don't make enough

time, for the important things in life, like family, community
and God.

The trick used to divert people's attention from their mission in
this world is thousands of years old. It was used by Pharaoh to try
and destroy the Jewish people in Egypt. "And the Egyptians made
the Children of Israel work with vigor." (Exodus 1:13) It is called
hard work or earning a living. On the one hand, earning one's own
living is a tremendous mitzvah as is stated in Psalms 128:2, "By
the toil of your hands you will eat. Praised are you and it will be
good for you." On the other hand, it is a tremendous diversion of
resources from one's main purpose.

Balance Between Spiritual and Material Activities

The balance between one's spiritual and material activities is the
subject of a well-known debate between Rabbi Yishmael and
Rabbi Shimon Bar Yochai in the Talmud Berachot 35b. The second
paragraph of the Shema, as we have already mentioned, contains
blessings from the Almighty. One of the blessings is that: "You
will gather your grain." Rabbi Yishmael understands this verse to
mean that people should earn their own living.

Rabbi Shimon Bar Yochai asks a logical question: "If we are to
be concerned with the harvest and our agricultural needs, when
will we ever have time to learn Torah?" He therefore explains the
verse as referring to a low-level blessing. We will be blessed with
sustenance but only through the sweat of our hands. The higher-
level blessing, however, is that, others will provide for us so that
we can engage totally in spiritual growth.[38]

The Talmud concludes this debate with the following comment:
'Many did like Rabbi Shimon Bar Yochai, but were not successful.
Many did like Rabbi Yishmael and were successful.' We have to

[38] See Tosafot, ibid.

try and follow the medium path of Rabbi Yishmael and balance the material and physical components of our lives.[39]

The Code of Jewish Law written by Rabbi Joseph Karo[40] in the sixteenth century formulates the law that a person should work for a living and also engage in learning Torah, the Torah learning being his main preoccupation.

In Orach Haim Chapter 156:1, he states the following:

> "After one's breakfast, one should go to work, because any Torah that is not accompanied by work will eventually lead to sin because poverty will make a person transgress God's will. Nevertheless a person should not make their work the main thing and their Torah learning the minor thing, but the Torah study should be the main focus and earning a living should be the minor focus. In this way a person will be successful in both."

In Parashat Terumah, God commanded the Jews to build Him a sanctuary and vessels, which included the Table and Menorah. We know that symbolically the Table in the Sanctuary represented the ability of the Jewish people to sustain themselves physically

---

[39] See this author's Jewish Law Meets Modern Challenges Volume 1 article entitled 'The Obligation to Learn Torah.'

[40] Rabbi Joseph Ben Ephraim Karo was born in Toledo, Spain in 1488, and died in Tzefat, Israel. He is also called Maran ("our master") or Ha-Mechaber ("the author," i.e. the halachic author par excellence). R. Karo left Spain in 1492 as a result of the Spanish expulsion of the Jews, and settled with his family in Turkey. In 1536, he emigrated to Israel and became the chief rabbi of Tzefat, an important center of Jewish learning and industry. His principal teacher in Tzefat was Rabbi Jacob Berab. R. Karo's magnum opus is his Beit Yosef ("House of Joseph"), an encyclopedic commentary on Rabbi Jacob Ben Asher's Tur, a halachic code. Bet Yosef presents an extensive survey of relevant halachic literature, from the Talmud down to works of R. Karo's contemporaries. R. Karo's halachic decisions were codified in his Shulchan Aruch (which was actually a digest of Bet Yosef). This work quickly became accepted throughout the Jewish world as halachically authoritative. Likewise, R. Karo's commentary on Maimonides' code, the Kessef Mishneh, is one of the standard commentaries on Maimonides' work. R. Karo was also a mystic. He left two responsa collections, Avkat Rochel and Bet Yosef.

and materially. The Menorah, however, symbolically represented Torah. The light of the Menorah symbolized the Light of the Torah. "Why is it then," asks the Siftei Cohen, "that the Table was placed first, before the Menorah? After all, the Menorah is more spiritually significant than the Table?"

The Mishnah (Avot 3:17) states that "If there is no flour there is no Torah." If there is no livelihood there can be no Torah. Therefore, first we place the Table, representing a livelihood, and then we put out the Menorah, representing Torah. But then, the Mishnah continues, "If there is no Torah, there is no livelihood. So why give the Table priority over the Menorah?

The Gaon of Vilna, in his commentary on Proverbs, comments on another Mishnah in Avot. The Mishnah states that "If there is no wisdom, there is no fear of God," and then it continues "If there is no fear of God, there is no wisdom." The Gaon explains this glaring dichotomy as follows: When we speak of chronological priorities, then wisdom has to precede fear of God because 'the ignoramus cannot be pious.' (Avot 2:5) Simply put one who doesn't know anything cannot be observant of God's laws. However, in terms of goals, priority is given to fear of God. In other words, if wisdom is not going to lead to action in the form of deeds, the wisdom is worthless. If a person learns Torah but does not have any other virtuous qualities, his learning is not worth much. The same is true here as well. In terms of chronological priorities, unless one establishes a viable means of supporting oneself there can be no Torah study. If one has to go around begging, he is not able to sit and learn. On the other side of the coin, if the physical welfare achieved doesn't lead to Torah (spiritual growth), if one is just accumulating money for the sake of physical growth only, then the money is worthless.

This is what the Torah is telling us: In the sanctuary, we first put the Table because 'If there is no food, there is no Torah.' Then we put the Menorah opposite the Table, because we have to realize that the Table's reason for being is to support the Menorah.

The Talmud in Shabbat 31a states that when a person reaches the world to come he is first asked the following three questions:

1. Did you fix times for Torah study?
2. Were you honest in business?
3. Did you look forward to the redemption?

These questions reflect the values that we are meant to prioritize.

The three questions listed reflect the ideals that we are to hold dearest: Study for personal and societal growth. Sanctify God's name and show your faith in God by being honest in business. Be a positive, cheerful person who lives with faith even when times are rough.

These are not quantitative questions but qualitative ones: One is not asked how many pages of Torah we have studied or how many topics we have mastered, but whether we were steadfast and committed to learning and made the Torah a fixed part of our lives. We are not asked how much money we earned or how vast a fortune we acquired, but whether we conducted our business with honesty. We are not asked how long we spent yearning for the redemption to come, but whether we hoped for the future redemption. Were we optimistic and hopeful about the future?

Judaism teaches us intense concern for the quality of our lives. It tries to distinguish between peripheral matters and those that truly determine the significance of our lives, and it tries to keep us focused on the ultimate significance.

Conclusion

There should be two main purposes in a Jew's life. They are:

1. To strive for individual perfection, in our character traits, in our relationship with God and in our relationships with fellow men.

2. To strive for societal perfection.

These two approaches have been the backbone of Jewish philosophy for millennia.

Chapter 3. Free Will & Inner Peace

Factors on which our level of free will depends.

Every intelligent human being has free will. Free will is a part of the human psyche. We all, however, differ as to the level of our free will, depending on the following:

a) Genetic factors account for a large part of our character traits, especially at an early age, before other influences have a chance to take effect.[41]

b) Our upbringing or conditioning is very important. This includes education. It cannot be emphasized enough how important a good Jewish education is for the survival of the next generation of vibrant Jews.

c) Environmental effects and influences.[42] These include peer pressure and influences from role models. Rambam states in Chapter 6:1 of Hilkhot De'ot:

---

[41] See Rambam De'ot 1:2. Today, unfortunately, our society has swung to the extreme in which genetic and psychological makeup are too commonly cited as reasons for moral lapses. The excuse for all kinds of deviant behavior is that the person involved cannot help it. He is forced by his genetic makeup to act this way. There is no question that genetics is an important ingredient in our physiological and psychological makeup, and is thus a factor in the way we behave, but to excuse unacceptable behavior in the name of genetics is absurd. We should never excuse a kleptomaniac of shoplifting by saying that this was an inherited trait, nor a murderer by saying that he could not help it, that this trait was part of his DNA. See the book <u>The Abuse Excuse and Other Cop-outs, Sob Stories, and Evasions of Responsibility</u> by Alan Dershowitz. He states: "at a deeper level, the abuse excuse is a symptom of a general abdication of responsibility by individuals, families, groups, and even nations. Its widespread acceptance is dangerous to the very tenets of democracy, which presupposes personal accountability for choices and actions...The abuse excuse is dangerous both in its narrow manifestation as a legal defense and in its broader manifestation as an abrogation of societal responsibility." It is also true that some individuals exist who are mentally ill inasmuch that they do not understand nor are capable of behaving in a manner which indicates that they can tell the difference between right and wrong.

[42] See Deuteronomy 20:18.

The natural tendency of a person is to be drawn after the thoughts and deeds of his friends and society. Therefore a person must associate with wise people...as King Solomon states: 'A person who associates with the wise will become wise...' and as the first verse of Psalms 1:1 state: 'Praised is a person who did not follow the advice of evil people and didn't stand in the presence of delinquents...'

We absorb a tremendous amount from the environment around us. It cannot be stressed enough how important it is to examine these environmental factors, especially when raising children, and also for ourselves.

In Jewish law, if two witnesses accuse someone of a capital offense, if that person is found guilty, these same witnesses are also the executioners. The reason for this is that they were the most influenced, since they witnessed the crime first-hand, the sight of which left a tremendous impact on them and may have lessened their sensitivity. To counteract any of the influence they may have received from witnessing the crime, they must be the ones to eradicate the evil.

In Exodus 32:7, Moses was up on Mount Sinai receiving the written and oral laws of the Torah when God informed him that he was to go back down to the people, as they had corrupted themselves by building and worshipping a calf. God told Moses that He would destroy the people and would make Moses the progenitor of a new nation. Moses defended the Jews successfully and God accepted his prayer to forgive the people.

Moses then descended the mountain with the two tablets of stone written by God in his hands. Moses was reunited with his disciple Joshua who heard a loud noise from the direction of the Israelite encampment below. They surmised as to the origins of the noise.

It was not until they got within sight of the camp that they realized that it was the sound of idolatry. Moses was so angry that he smashed the tablets. We can see from this that sight and first hand experiences leave much more of an impact than just hearing about an episode. Moses did not get angry before he actually witnessed with his own eyes the depraved behavior of the people.

The Torah, at the beginning of Exodus (2:21), relates Moses' sojourning with Yitro in the following way: "Vayoel Moshe...." The Talmud, Nedarim 65a, explains that Moses made an oath to his father-in-law. There is some speculation as to the content of this oath. The Midrash states that the oath was that he would raise one of his children in the faith of Yitro, his father-in-law, who was then an idol worshiper. Rabbi Dessler then asks the obvious question. How could the great and holy Moses take such an oath? He answers that Moses never really took an oath, nor made any commitments, but the fact that he lived so long with his father-in-law, the idolater, was as if he took an oath, for he virtually guaranteed a tremendously bad impact on his children.

This signifies the power of the environment. Slowly, one adapts to the situation one is in and becomes morally and ethically numb. Recall what happened to Lot, nephew and brother-in-law of Abraham. How could Lot, who was raised in Abraham's house at a very high moral and ethical level, go to live in Sodom? The answer the commentaries state was his great love for money. The Torah tells us (Genesis 13:10; 11) that he saw the land was verdant and good for cattle. He was willing to go and live in Sodom, confident in his ability to resist temptation, because that was where he could earn the most money. Two of his daughters intermarried with the inhabitants of the land and were destroyed with them. Lot himself not only adapted to their evil ways, but eventually was appointed a judge over them. One of the good traits that he still nurtured was hospitality. This is what saved him in the end.

No-one can be sure of his or her ability to resist temptation, or the blandishments of society around them. Every morning, in the blessings we recite from the beginning of the prayer book, we beseech God to "Keep me far away today and always from an evil person, from the evil inclination, from an evil friend and evil neighbor, etc." We also pray to God not to test us. The commentaries say that an evil neighbor is much worse than an evil friend, because the neighbor is nearly always present and the influence is insidious. Whereas we can choose our friends, we cannot always choose our neighbors. However strong our personalities are, we are all influenced to some extent by other people around us, by the neighborhood we live in, by the programs we watch on TV, by the magazines and periodicals we read, and the radio stations we listen to.

The Talmud, Berachot 29a, stresses the idea that people should not trust in their innate propensities for good versus the power of the environment. "Don't trust yourself until the day of your death." As proof of this statement the Talmud cites the story of Yochanan, the High Priest, reputedly the holiest and most respected person of his time who served God in the holy temple for eighty years and eventually succumbed to heresy.

Free Will

The Torah in Genesis (1:27), states that human-beings were created in the image of God. Rambam[43] comments that, among all living creatures, humans alone are endowed with morality, reason and free will. Only humans can know and love God and can hold spiritual communion with Him. It is in this sense that the Torah describes humanity as having been created in the Divine image.

Rabbi Hanina in the Talmud Berachot 33 makes an exceptionally powerful statement: "Everything is in the hands of heaven except for the fear of heaven."

---

[43] Hilkhot Teshuvah 5:1.

In running our lives, many of our choices are in our hands. The Almighty God in His wisdom gave us the greatest gift possible, freedom - freedom to choose and even to disobey Him.

It is customary that on Friday nights and on the eves of festivals 'Yigdal' is sung in the Synagogue after the evening service. 'Yigdal' consists of Rambam's codification of the thirteen principles of faith,[44] which was set to a tune by one of his students and which forms the basis of our belief system.

In the 'Yigdal' we mention that God rewards a pious person according to his or her conduct and punishes an evil person according to his or her misdeeds. Without the gift of free will, we would all be comparable to robots or machinery. You don't reward your computer for performing a task, neither would you punish it for not performing. It has no other choice. The fact that we believe that God rewards and punishes ultimately means that we believe in this concept of free will.

Rambam[45] declares that all humans have free choice. He then explains one of the notable exceptions, the case of Pharaoh. The Torah[46] tells us that God hardened Pharaoh's heart. This is taken by the Rambam to mean that God removed Pharaoh's freewill and his ability to repent. He goes on to explain that freewill should not be taken for granted. God can and does remove the ability to make different choices from a person whom He wants to utterly destroy, as was the case with Pharaoh. Pharaoh had crossed a line in terms of his barbaric behavior toward the defenseless Israelites in his kingdom. God did not allow him to repent.

---

[44] The Thirteen Principles are: 1) God is ever-present and is in control. 2) God is one. 3) God is not bound by a physical shape. 4) God is eternal. 5) There is no other God. 6) God knows what people think. 7) Moses' prophecy is true. 8) Moses was the master of all the prophets. 9) The Torah was given from heaven. 10) The Torah is immutable. 11) God rewards the righteous and punishes the wicked. 12) The Messiah will come. 13) The dead will arise.

[45] Hilkhot Teshuvah 6:3.

[46] Exodus 10:20.

The Bet Halevy,[47] however, has a different perspective on the issue of why God hardened Pharaoh's heart. After witnessing the power of the first few plagues, Pharaoh was overwhelmed. He found it impossible to continue to resist God's command to let the Hebrews go. God hardened his heart, i.e. gave him the ability to regain his free choice and the possibility to choose to disobey God, should he wish to. God did not remove Pharaoh's free will. On the contrary He returned it to him. According to the Bet Halevy's perspective God would never remove anyone's free will, not even to exact retribution.

Rabbi Eliyahu Dessler,[48] in his book <u>Strive for Truth</u> gives a very illuminating perspective of the different levels of free will. He discusses 'the point of free will.' This is the point at which a person is still debating the issues in his mind. Rabbi Dessler gives an analogy of two armies in battle. The point of conflict is at the front line. Behind the front lines there is no battle. It is clear to whom the land belongs until the front line changes. We all internally debate the various issues that affect us on a continuous basis. This is where the front line of our free will is located. Issues that we have already decided are not usually reexamined, and therefore we have no free choice over them. We have consigned them to habit. That is what habits are, things that have become second nature that we do not even think about. One can have good habits and bad habits. With respect to habits, it is as if our hearts have been hardened.

A person who constantly reevaluates his or her habits still has the power to change them and therefore retains free will. A person who does not reevaluate his or her habits will not have free will concerning them. He or she will be stuck in a rut of his or her own making.

---

[47] In his commentary on the Torah of the same name.
[48] See glossary.

A person who was raised with good habits that were never reevaluated will not receive the same reward as someone who was not raised the same way, but who acquired these habits out of choice. As Rambam[49] states, "In a place that a penitent stands, a righteous individual cannot stand." Rambam explains this statement as follows: A person who has tasted sin and keeps away, despite the knowledge of how pleasant it was, is greater than a person who has never tasted sin and therefore does not know what he or she is missing.

Reevaluate Habits Frequently

Another possible explanation for the greatness of a penitent (baal teshuvah) is that a righteous individual, who has been raised that way from youth, has formed habits and does not normally question them. He or she never made a conscious choice. Everything was handed to him or her on a silver platter. A penitent however, has made a conscious, painful choice to alter his or her old habits. This is why it is good to reevaluate one's actions and receive a reward for re-accepting the commandments afresh, as opposed to just performing them from habit.

For example, a person who was brought up to keep Shabbat and has never really questioned whether to continue to keep Shabbat, has not really made a free-will choice. A person who did not have the same upbringing and made a conscious choice to observe Shabbat laws is therefore on a higher level.

Issues that are still undecided or that we haven't yet examined are still within the boundaries of our free will. Those that have already been examined and decided are not considered to be within our free will if they are not going to be re-examined. Thus, our point of free will is constantly changing. As we grow or diminish spiritually, so too the scope of our choices changes.

---

[49] Hilkhot Teshuvah 7:4.

There is a beautiful story that illustrates this idea. Rabbi Saadiah Gaon, famous 8th century Babylonian leader and sage, was visiting a small town and stayed at the local hotel. The staff was unaware of the identity of this illustrious personage and, while they treated him courteously, nobody went out of their way to do the small extras that are usually performed for famous guests. While his room was clean and in perfect order, it did not have the best view and was some distance from the bathroom.

Just before he went to check out of the hotel, he heard a knock on the door. He opened it and to his amazement there was the owner of the establishment in tears. "Rabbi," he pleaded, "please forgive me for the poor service. I did not know who you were. Please, Rabbi, accept my humble apologies for all the inconveniences that you suffered."

The Rabbi shook his head in disbelief. "Everything was fine, my good man. Don't fret. The room was clean. The bed was comfortable. I was satisfied with the service."

"Rabbi," the man repeated "if I had known who you were, I would have treated you much better."

It was the Rabbi's turn to break down and cry. The hotel owner looked on in amazement. Slowly his sobs dissipated. "Why are you so upset, Rabbi?" he asked in wonderment.

"You taught me something," answered the sage "I am crying to God for forgiveness, because I should have served Him better previously if I had known then what I now know about His greatness."

Everything is in the hands of Heaven except for the fear of Heaven

The Talmud[50] mentions a very famous dictum, 'Everything is in the hand of heaven except for the fear of heaven.' The sages of the Talmud learned this principle from the verse in Deuteronomy 10, "What does God want from you? Only for you to fear Him." The only thing that we have the free will to do is to fear Him. Whether we will be rich or poor, tall or short, handsome or ugly, has already been decided, and is usually beyond our absolute control.

The only thing that is within our total control is our freewill. Decisions on whether to be moral, ethical monotheists are totally within our control.

Quality of Life

Each person makes daily choices regarding the quality of his or her life. We choose our thoughts and behavior. If our choices are elevated thoughts and actions, which include Torah study, trust in the Almighty, love, kindness and good deeds, we will live elevated and fulfilling lives. If we choose hostile, aggressive, depressing and self-pitying thoughts and destructive behavior, our life will be full of pain and contention.

The path of the Torah is a path of life, compassion, mercy, love, happiness and joy. To travel this path one must integrate and internalize the beautiful concepts, which create the elevated and transcendental human being. Many people can quote the right concepts but have difficulty applying them.

In Deuteronomy 30:19 we are commanded to choose life. "I have set before you the blessing and the curse; choose life." Like any good parent, God wants us to make the right decisions but has empowered us to make them for ourselves. The power of free will

---

[50] Megillah 25a.

gives us superiority over the animal kingdom and enables us to grow in awareness and understanding. However, there are times when we do not utilize this great gift. Instead of responding logically and constructively to various situations, we react instinctively, as if we had no choice in the matter. For example, one' might think to him or herself: "Whenever a family member fails to cooperate with my request for help I feel unloved and unloving. I often shout angrily or seethe in silent resentment." Or one may think that: "Whenever someone criticizes me, I feel like a total failure and brood about it for hours." We might think that such responses are 'natural' and unavoidable and that we cannot help but react as we did. But this implies that we are more like robots than a free-willed human being.

When we give people, places, and things the power to pull us into a state of negativity, then we have at that moment given away our independence and our power of choice. To break these automatic habit patterns it is necessary to identify them and to work at developing the intellectual and emotional honesty that is necessary for growth. Then we regain our free will.

Imagine two escalators in front of you: the first leads upwards literally to an elevated existence; happiness, inspiration, purpose goodness etc. The second leads downwards a slippery slope towards nihilism and self-destruction.

These two escalators are described in the Torah in a number of places including at the beginning of Parashat Re'eh[51]:

See, I present before you today a blessing and a curse. The blessing: that you listen to the commandments of Hashem, your God ... And the curse: If you do not hearken to the commandments of Hashem...

---

[51] Deuteronomy 11:26

Rashi[52] states the principle of 'mitzvah goreret mitzvah' and 'averah goreret averah[53]' 'one good deed leads to another and one bad deed leads to another.' Deeds are like chain reactions and like slippery slopes.

'No man is an island' we are social beings and need positive peer support. We and our children and families need to be part of frameworks: schools, friends, groups of righteous people; communities of good decent people where goodness is a way of life. We need to be involved daily in mitzvot and good deeds and get on the upward bound escalator using our freewill to choose life.

---

[52] Deuteronomy 22:8
[53] Deuteronomy 21:22

Notes

Chapter 4. The Human Personality

On a very basic level Human beings are comprised of the physical, emotional, mental and spiritual.

Have you ever stood in front of a mirror and, while staring at your reflection, wondered who you really are? You are, for all intents and purposes, the sum of the above. But the core of every person is his or her character or personality. This is probably the most complex part of any human being. The personality can be thought of as reflecting all the different traits of the person. These are usually fixed at a very early age, and one is then stuck in the rut of habit with only minor changes occurring later on. There are very few people who are able to make major changes in their personalities at a later stage in life.

The Vilna Gaon in his excellent book <u>Even Shelemah</u> states that "A person's mission in this world is to perfect his or her traits, and personality." He emphasizes that enabling us to achieve this perfection is the main goal of the Torah. He states that it is easier to learn the whole Talmud than to change even one of a person's traits. We all know how difficult it is to learn the whole Talmud. Besides being in Aramaic and consisting of very intricate legal arguments, it is also very long. Assuming that a person would learn one page each day, it would take seven years to complete.

Most people don't even give a fleeting thought to their personality traits, the most critical aspect of their lives.

All our thoughts are rooted in our traits. All our actions are rooted in our traits. The traits govern the way we think and act. We ought to pay more attention to them. They are the important ingredients that make up who we really are.

External Motivators

What techniques can be applied to motivate someone? This is an age-old question that is especially pertinent today, as any supervisor of employees or any parent with children knows. Many children and a lot of adults are lethargic, lazy and not motivated. Obviously, a person who is not motivated will not achieve anything, so the first step has to be to encourage and coax them into action.

Generally speaking, there are two kinds of motivators: the 'carrot' and the 'stick.' These are very broad concepts. The carrot denotes pleasurable enticements and inducements, and the stick denotes painful consequences that can be applied to discourage specific actions.

At the beginning of the Torah, we find that God motivated Adam by giving him a glorious, unspoiled world, as well as the power and prestige of being in charge. When Adam felt alone, God provided him with a mate. This was the carrot approach, designed to motivate Adam in a positive, pleasurable way. When Adam rebelled against God, he was thrown out of his ideal setting and was left to fend for himself. This was the stick.

These motivators are external motivators because they depend on external factors. In today's society, a worker may be motivated by a profit-sharing plan, the promise of a pay increase, or the thought of promotion. The threats of demotion, loss of salary or benefits, or finally his or her job are some modern-day equivalents of a stick.

Internal Motivators

The Torah in Genesis 2:7 refers to the creation of man as "God formed man from the earth." The word used for formed in Hebrew (vayitzer) has two 'yods' as opposed to the usual one 'yod'. Ba'al Haturim comments that the two 'yods' represent two opposing inclinations, one impelling man to good and the other to evil. These inclinations are the internal motivators of man.

In Deuteronomy, Chapter 6:5, in the second line of the 'Shema,' the Torah tells us: 'And you will love the Lord your God with all your heart, all your soul and all your might.' The word used for heart in the Hebrew (lebabcha) has two letter 'bets,' whereas etymologically it should only have one (libcha). Rashi explains that the two 'bets' represent the two inclinations that are constantly vying for control over us. We have to love God with both of them.

The Midrash[54] points out seemingly contradictory statements made in the account of the creation of man. In Chapter 1:27, the Bible describes Adam as having been created in the image of God and in Chapter 2:7 he is described as having been created from the dust of the ground. The answer given is that mankind possesses both these qualities: the spiritual, denoted by being created in the image of God, and the base physical characteristics, denoted by being created from the dust. We have to chart a course between them.

We face a constant struggle between temptation and conscience. We can compare the different inclinations to the gears of an automobile, the good inclination being analogous to the forward gears that propel the car forward, and the evil inclination analogous to the reverse gears propelling the car backward.

There is also another gear: neutral - escape, do nothing, retreat from society, don't do good or bad. This, by the way, is today's most widely-held misconception of what the definition of a good person is. If you ask around, the most common answer invariably is that a good person is someone who has never hurt anyone.

---

[54] Bereshit 12:8.

The Evil Inclination

There is an enormously thought-provoking piece in the Talmud[55] that quotes a verse in Nechemiah 9, which discusses events that took place after the destruction of the first temple.

The sages, under the direction of Ezra Hasofer, one of the leaders of the Great Assembly (Anshei Knesset Hagedolah), saw that despite the great destruction wrought upon the Jewish people by the Babylonian onslaught, the evil inclination was still alive and well. They prayed to God to order the evil inclination to cease all its activities, fearful lest the new temple (Beth Hamikdash) they were then building would go the same way as the first. The Talmud describes their prayer as follows: "You only gave us an evil inclination in order to receive a reward (for serving God despite the blandishments of the inclination). We want neither the evil inclination nor the reward."

The result of the sages' prayer was unforeseen by them. All normal worldly activity stopped, during which, in the words of the Talmud, "they searched for a fresh egg in the whole of Israel and they couldn't find one." They saw that, as a result of their actions, even hens stopped laying eggs and people would stop having children, building houses, and engaging in commerce, and all mundane activity would come to a standstill.

The Talmud ends this story by saying that, instead of abolishing the evil inclination entirely the sages halved its power to allow the world to thrive in its present form.

The Midrash, in Genesis 9:7, reinforces the idea that the evil inclination, which corresponds to a person's untamed passions and desires, is not intrinsically evil and therefore should be controlled but not destroyed. Without the desires and ego, which emanate

---

[55] Yoma 69b.

from the evil inclination, humans would never be motivated enough to provide for their basic physical needs. Without it, a human being would never marry, have children, build a house, or engage in trade. It is only when the evil inclination gets out of hand that it becomes the cause of harm.

The Talmud in Kiddushin 30b states that God said "I created the evil inclination and I created the Torah as a spice for it." The Torah is conceived as ordering, guiding and disciplining the untamed instinctual natural urges. Just as certain foods are not palatable without spices, so too without Torah, a person will not be able to harness, control, and productively utilize his or her inclination.

The Talmud[56] states that unless it is checked and controlled, the evil inclination will grow by force of habit. A person starts moving in the wrong direction and gets habituated to that lifestyle, which then acquires a momentum of its own. At first, the evil inclination can be thought of resembling the thread of a spider's web, but at the end it is like a stout rope. It starts off by being a guest and ends off by making itself the master of the house.

Greatness does not render a person immune from the power of the evil inclination, on the contrary, the greater the person, the greater his or her evil inclination.[57] This is necessary in order to keep the person's choices open and one's free will balanced. It is surprising to find that a person who has done many evil deeds has less of an inclination for evil. Since his/her habits and deeds are evil, he/she does not have to be constantly bombarded by the evil inclination the opposite is true for a person who is continually involved in doing good.

The Talmud[58] illustrates the greater power of the evil inclination as a motivator than the good inclination in the following story:

---

[56] Sukkah 52a.
[57] Ibid.
[58] Baba Metzia 84a.

'Resh Lakish was a well-known leader of a band of robbers. One day, while walking on the bank of the river, he noticed what appeared to be a beautiful woman bathing on the other bank of the river. He drew nearer to get a better glimpse of her beauty. With supreme effort, he made a tremendous leap and drew near to the woman. To his utter chagrin, it was a man, and no ordinary man, but Rabbi Yochanan, a leader of the generation. The famous Rabbi had noticed the colossal vault Resh Lakish had taken and asked him the reason for his extraordinary behavior. Resh Lakish sheepishly answered that he had mistaken the good Rabbi for a woman and he was coming closer for a better look. Rabbi Yochanan answered that if it was beauty Resh Lakish was looking for, he would introduce him to his sister, but only on the condition that Resh Lakish would turn over a new leaf and devote his extraordinary strength and vitality to the learning and practicing of Torah. Resh Lakish readily agreed. The Rabbi's family members were noted for their beauty. Resh Lakish wanted to return to the opposite bank to collect his weapons. He tried once more to leap across the river. There was a loud splash. This time he didn't make it and fell in. The commentaries explain that once he had taken upon himself the responsibilities of the Torah, he was automatically weakened.'

We also see this concept in the prayer of 'Al Hanissim,' which is added on Chanukah to thank God for the tremendous military victory of a small band of Maccabees against the Syrian Greek forces: "And You gave the strong into the hands of the weak." Why were the Maccabees considered weaker that the Greeks? The commentaries explain that those who are righteous feel physically weaker than others, as they are burdened by the yoke of the commandments.

The Wilderness of Existence

The fourth book of the Bible, Numbers, is 'Bemidbar'[59] in Hebrew, which means 'In the Wilderness.' This book[60] marks the transition of the Children of Israel from a wild, demoralized and disorganized band of ex-slaves into a highly-disciplined, motivated and holy nation. The wilderness is an area that is savage and untamed. Primitive impulses dominate such a place. In the wilderness, the Israelites succumbed to their worst impulses: cowardice,[61] lack of faith in God,[62] jealousy,[63] and lust.[64]

A person who cannot control his or her evil inclination is likened to being in a wilderness. Such a person will never achieve inner peace. A person who is unsure of what his or her goals are, and lacks purpose, can be thought of as wandering around aimlessly in a wilderness. Without the Torah as our guide, we would all have to go through a period of 'wilderness' to find ourselves and to find purpose.

---

[59] The English name 'Numbers' is taken from the second verse, in which God commanded Moses to number the Israelites.

[60] The Ramban delineates the central theme of each of the five books. Bereshit (Bereshit): Creation, the selection of the forefathers and the giving to them of the land of Israel. Shemot (Exodus): From slavery to freedom; the Ten Commandments and the residing of the Shechinah (Divine Presence) in the midst of the Israelite camp. Vayikra (Leviticus): The attainment of Kedushah (sanctity) resulting in a closeness to God. Devarim (Deuteronomy): also called the Mishneh Torah - The second Torah because Moses reviews the past in preparation for his death and the imminent entry of the Israelites into the land.

[61] Numbers 14:1. The ten spies came back with a negative report about the land of Israel and sowed fear into the hearts of the people who then wept bitterly.

[62] Numbers 14:11.

[63] Numbers 16:3. Korach, Moses' own cousin fomented trouble against him, based on envy.

[64] Numbers 25:1.

The Three Powerful, Dangerous but Necessary Motivators

The Mishnah in Pirke Avot 4:21 quotes Rabbi Eliezer Hakappar, who lists three of the worst character traits: "Jealousy, lust and honor-seeking remove a person from the world." (He or she will self-destruct.) However these three traits are also some of the greatest motivators known to man and are necessary in a moderate form.

The complete eradication of these three traits would threaten man's survival. The world as we know it would cease to exist, and would probably not survive another generation. On the other hand, if these traits were allowed to run out of control, the world would also be morally, ethically and spiritually destroyed. The Torah, therefore, contains rules and regulations to keep these three traits under strict control.

A. Jealousy

'Keeping up with the Jones' is the motivation for the lives that many of us lead. Its core is jealousy. The Torah is replete with tales of jealousy. Cain and Abel, Joseph and his brothers, Korah and Moses, King Ahab and Naboth's vineyard, to mention but a few, are all classic tales of jealousy. Jealousy is a motivator so extremely powerful that it can sometimes lead to committing three terrible crimes: murder, adultery and robbery. It is no coincidence that the Ten Commandments (Exodus 20:2 & Deuteronomy 5:6) end with the prohibition of coveting one's neighbor's possessions. The Torah also prohibits the desire of one's neighbor's property. (Deuteronomy 5:17)

The so called 'evil eye' is the eye of a greedy and jealous person. The Talmud[65] discusses the antidote for the evil eye. It says to say

---

[65] Berachot 20a.

a verse from Jacob's blessing of Joseph,[66] implying that Joseph was successful in countering the effects of the evil eye[67] From this we can infer that the evil eye is jealousy. Joseph successfully survived the jealousy of his brothers and the selfish desires of Potiphar's wife. Although these episodes had negative impacts on his life, he successfully overcame all obstacles and achieved fame and fortune. He finally married Potiphar's daughter and financially supported his brothers and their families.

The Talmud continues by asking how Joseph was successful in countering the effects of the evil eye and answers, "The eyes that did not partake from that which did not belong to them - the evil eye has no power over." Joseph did not partake of any visual pleasure from Potiphar's wife and had no illicit desire for her. He was thus spared from other people's jealousy and desire. If we are not jealous, or covetous of other people's property, then other people's jealousies and desires will have no effect on us.

The Shulchan Aruch[68] quotes an interesting law that the owner of the house and not his or her guest should break and allocate bread to people around the dinner table. The reason given is that the host has a 'good' eye. In this context, this means that the host will allocate generous helpings of bread, while a guest may be hesitant to give away too much of his host's bread. We see that the 'good' eye is that of a generous person. If we assume that an 'evil' eye is the opposite of a good eye, this law reveals to us its definition of miserliness and jealousy.

On the other hand, a certain type of jealousy is highly recommended. In the words of the Talmud,[69] 'Jealousy of scribes increases wisdom.' It is desirable to be jealous of the deeds, good qualities

---

66   Bereshit 49:22.

67   Bereshit 48:16.

68   Code of Jewish Law Orach Haim 167:14 Mishnah Berurah 74.

69   Baba Batra 21a.

and character of righteous people. This will encourage a person to raise his or her sights and perform more good deeds.[70]

B. Desire

There are three major spheres of human activity. Some are mandatory, some are optional, and some are prohibited.

Necessary Desires / Pleasures.

Eating, sleeping and conjugal relations all fall within the category of necessary desires/pleasures. A person has to eat, sleep and procreate in order for the human species to survive. However, it is ironic that it is with regard to these very basic and productive functions that the Torah contains an abundance of regulations.

Eating

While we are commanded to eat, albeit indirectly, from the command to guard our souls very carefully (Deuteronomy 4:15), there are a myriad of laws concerning what, how, and when we should eat. All the laws of kashrut and blessings over food are basically to regulate and sanctify this primary instinct.

Is a person allowed to eat more than he or she requires in order to live a healthy life? Both Rambam and Ramban rule in the negative. Rambam (De'ot 4:2) advises us to cease eating when we are still a quarter empty, in order to promote good health. He writes that the majority of illnesses are caused by overeating or by eating unhealthy foods. We should eat to live and not live to eat.

Ramban, in his famous commentary on the Torah in Parashat

---

[70] On the other hand it can also have the disastrous effect of depressing the person whose sights have been raised to unattainable standards. A person must have realistic short and long-term goals.

Kedoshim (Leviticus 19:2), explains the Torah's enjoinder to be holy as a mitzvah to abstain from excesses in any desire.

"The Torah has admonished us against immorality and forbidden foods, but permitted sexual intercourse between husband and wife, and the eating of certain meat and wine. People of desire could consider this to mean that they are permitted to be passionately addicted to sexual intercourse with their spouse, to be among alcoholics and gluttonous eaters of flesh, and to speak freely all profanities, since these prohibitions have not been expressly mentioned in the Torah. Thus one could become a sordid person within the permissible realm of the Torah! Therefore, having listed the matters which God prohibited altogether, Scripture followed them up by a general command that we practice moderation, even in matters that are permitted.

One should minimize sexual intercourse, except in the fulfillment of the mitzvah. One should also sanctify oneself to self-restraint by using wine and other alcoholic beverages in small quantities, just as the Bible calls a Nazirite holy for abstaining from wine and strong drink. A person should remember the evils mentioned in the Torah of drinking wine, as in the stories of Noah and Lot. Likewise, one should guard one's mouth and tongue from being defiled by excessive food and by vulgar speach. One should purify oneself in this respect until one reaches the degree known as complete self-restraint. Cleanliness of hands and body (personal hygiene), are also included in this precept.

God's main intent is to warn us that we should be physically clean and ritually pure, and separated from the common people who soil themselves with luxuries and unseemly things."

In summary, Ramban explains this verse, which contains the admonition to be holy, as advocating moderation in the following six areas which are otherwise permitted by the Torah:

a) Sex, even in a permitted form should be controlled.
b) Drinking alcoholic beverages should be done with moderation.
c) Gluttonous desires to overeat should be calmed.
d) One should employ decency in speech, curbing one's tongue from uttering profanities.
e) Physical hygiene and cleanliness is a prerequisite for holiness.
f) One should exercise social discretion, including separation from coarse and vulgar individuals who constantly engage in gratifying their desires.

Sleep

There are laws of when to sleep, how long, and even what posture to adopt when sleeping. The body and mind need downtime to regenerate, but as with other pleasures, too much sleep can seriously weaken the body and be dangerous to one's health. Muscles can degenerate and a person may get bedsores and become weak from over-sleeping. Rambam (De'ot 4:4) recommends that a person sleep eight hours a night in order to remain healthy. Some people may require more and some less. A person should sleep on the left side for at least the first half of the night, in order to aid their digestion. A person should never sleep on the back or front, as it is a disrespectful posture. A person should not sleep in the day, especially after a heavy meal. The gases from the stomach filter into the brain.

Sex

The marital laws prohibit sex outside of a halachically-constituted marriage. Even sex within marriage is regulated. The laws concerning marital relations leave nothing to the imagination. Everything is codified. Even though certain pleasures are allowed, even mandatory, God in his wisdom does not want us to over-indulge, even within a legitimate marriage, hence the laws of Niddah and Mikvah. These laws basically prohibit a wife and husband from partaking in any sexual activity for a period of approximately twelve days a month, depending on a number of factors that are beyond the scope of this book.

During these very permissive times, it is hard to imagine the holiness and restraint exhibited by the very special people who keep these laws. To live in the same room with one's legitimate partner and not to engage in the marital act or any other physical act of endearment requires tremendous restraint, bordering on the superhuman.

Needless to say, a couple who observes these laws goes through a honeymoon period every month.

Material Wealth

The desire for material things and wealth can fall into all three categories discussed above. A person may be motivated to amass more of a fortune, or to purchase more material belongings in order to keep up with those around him. This is rooted in jealousy. If the person wants to amass these items because they are pleasurable, this instinct is rooted in desire. If the person wants to amass material wealth for the sake of prestige, this would come under the third category of status seeking.

The Torah by no means denigrates material wealth. To the contrary, all the Torah blessings for keeping God's laws, such as those in the Shema, are expressed as material abundance. Rambam asks the question: (Hilkhot Teshuvah 9:1) "Why are the blessings in the Torah all physical and why doesn't the Torah explicitly promise paradise and other extraterrestrial rewards?" He answers that the physical blessings mentioned in the Torah are to enable the recipient to perform more mitzvot, and to climb spiritually.

Material wealth is a blessing from God as long as it is recognized for what it is, the means to an end. Material wealth should be used to better enhance a person's ability to serve God, as opposed to being an end in itself. The Torah[71] predicts and warns that eventually the Jews will become wealthy and forget God. There is also a special mitzvah to remember daily that our wealth and might come from God.[72] In the Shema[73] we are commanded to love God with our wealth. The Talmud[74] states that a person's character can be recognized in three things - his or her wallet, cup and anger - that is, where and why they spend money, why they celebrate, and why they get angry. The tests of wealth are:

a) What is it spent on?
b) Does one still thank and acknowledge God for the gift of wealth, or does it make a person proud and withdrawn from God?

Judaism has never viewed poverty as a spiritual advantage. To the contrary, the constant worrying over how to make ends meet and the constant daily grind to just exist do not allow people to focus on their spirituality. The Midrash[75] emphasizes that a poor person is like a dead person. For, just as a dead person cannot elevate

---

[71] Deuteronomy 32:15.
[72] Deuteronomy 8:17-18.
[73] Deuteronomy 6:5.
[74] Erubin 65b.
[75] Midrash Rabbah Exodus 5:4.

themselves spiritually by doing good deeds, so too a poor person who is so involved in earning his daily bread will not have the time or energy for worthy actions.

Further, the Torah does not encourage a monastic lifestyle. We are encouraged to intermingle with the rest of humanity, taking care that our values influence theirs and not *vice versa*. We see this idea of the importance of being involved with worldly matters in the prayer of Abraham when he pleaded with God to save the evil city of Sodom. Abraham pleads (Genesis 18:23) that if there are a certain number of righteous people in the midst of the city, then God should spare the city. Note the words 'in the midst of the city.' The righteous have to be in the midst of everything if they are going to exert a positive influence on society.

The Torah emphasizes the fact that our forefathers were wealthy. In fact, when Jacob had to run away from his brother Esav, leaving all his possessions behind, the Torah (Genesis 29:11) tells us that when he saw his cousin Rachel he wept. One of the reasons Rashi advances to explain his weeping was that he had arrived penniless and couldn't afford to give her gifts, unlike his father's servant Eliezer, who had arrived with ten fully-laden camels bearing gifts for his mother Rebecca and her family.

The Talmud (Berachot 57b) clearly expresses the thought that aesthetics is desirable for the service of God. 'Three things heighten the awareness of man: a beautiful place to live, a pretty wife,[76] and elegant furniture.' This heightened awareness should be utilized to draw one closer to God.

---

[76] The Torah stresses that the wives of our forefathers were beautiful. As for our mother Rachel, it stresses her beauty twice. The commentaries discuss two kinds of beauty, external and internal. Internal beauty is called grace. King Solomon does say in Eshet Chayil (Proverbs 31:30), which is read at the kiddush table every Friday night, 'Grace is a lie, and beauty is vanity. A woman who fears God, she will be praised.' He is talking about these values by themselves, but if the woman had beauty as well as fear of God, that beauty is praiseworthy.

Rabenu Tam, a grandson of Rashi and a famous twelfth century rabbi and Tosafist was known to keep four gold coins on the table in front of him when he learned Torah, so as to give himself the freedom from worry that is so necessary to succeed in advanced Torah scholarship.

Yes, material possessions are important. However, we must not forget that the bottom line of all our physical possessions is to enhance our service of God.

C. Status-Seeking / Ego Trips

Social climbing has become an accepted part of life. We are all trying to climb the rungs of the socio-economic ladder. If a person's sole intent in doing anything is to receive more honor from others, this type of selfish honor-seeking can destroy the person.

The Bible[77] relates a tragic argument between Korach and his cousin Moses. Korach was not happy that Moses and Aaron had secured top positions in the administration and that another cousin had been elevated over him. Seeking more honor for himself, he started a very dangerous rebellion against Moses' leadership, attracting many important individuals to his cause. The result of his grab for power was not advantageous to him, but rather served to reinforce Moses' leadership. From being a very important and wealthy personage in his own right, and a cousin of Moses, he was swallowed alive into the bowels of the earth, coming to an ignominious end.

Adonijah was the fourth oldest son of King David. Even though his father was still alive, he would hire sprinters to run ahead of his chariot, proclaiming him as the future King of Israel.[78] Needless to say, he was not chosen to be King David's successor.

---

[77] Numbers 6:1.
[78] Kings I. 1:5.

Yereboam ben Nevat was the head of the Sanhedrin in the days of King Solomon. He was chosen by God to be King over the northern kingdom of Israel when the ten tribes broke away from the rule of Rehoboam, the son of King Solomon. One of Yereboam's first acts was to institute calf worship.[79] He reasoned that if the citizens of his northern kingdom of Israel would go to the Temple in Jerusalem three times a year[80] and see the greatness of the King of Judah, they might come back with the idea that he, Yereboam, was not the real king.[81]

The Talmud[82] goes further in castigating Yereboam's ego. It states that God appeared to Yereboam and asked him to repent (do teshuvah). Yereboam was promised that if he would repent God would accompany him and King David in Paradise. Yereboam's response was startling: "Who will go first, me or David?" When told that King David would lead the way, Yereboam refused to do teshuvah. This illustrates the destructive power of the ego.

The Midrash[83] states that the more a person chases after a position of honor, the more the position eludes him or her. The converse is also true. The more a person runs away from a position of honor, the more it chases him or her. The Midrash gives different examples of those who ran away from honor. They include some of our greatest leaders: Moses, our greatest prophet tried his best not to accept the task of leading the Jewish people. He made every possible excuse. Saul, the first King of Israel, was also an unwilling leader. He was an overly humble person who could not believe it when Samuel the prophet announced that he would be the first

---

[79] Kings 1, 12:32.
[80] According to biblical law, every Jew had to go to the Sanctuary and, later on, to the Temple in Jerusalem three times a year, on Passover (Pesach), the Festival of Weeks (Shavuot) and Tabernacles (Sukkot).
[81] This was because only Kings who were descended from King David were allowed to sit in the courtyard of the temple. Everyone else had to stand, including Jereboam, the King of the Northern Kingdom of Israel.
[82] Sanhedrin 102a.
[83] Tanchuma 3.

King of Israel. He also lacked the strength of character to resist the wishes of the people maybe because of his lack of self-esteem.[84]

And yet, a certain amount of ego is important for our mental health. We all need to feel self-worth. The difference between self-respect and pride is that pride presents a false view of the person's worth. Self-respect on the other hand, is people acknowledging their true worth with total honesty. The difference between self-respect and humility is that people with true humility while knowing their self-worth ascribes all their strengths to God.

The Talmud[85] offers an interesting insight to this topic. It discusses the descending worth of each generation, relative to the previous one. One of the examples it brings is that humility and fear of sin are nonexistent today, since the death of Rabbi Judah the Prince, the editor of the Mishnah some nineteen hundred years ago. Rabbi Joseph objected, "Don't say that humility is dead, for I am still alive." And Rabbi Nachman interjected, "Don't say that fear of sin is dead, for I am still alive." This seems to be a very strange way to express humility. In fact it smacks totally of pride. If we understand pride to be a mistaken sense of self-worth and humility as the real state, we can understand that Rabbi Joseph was not boasting, but rather stating a fact. Since he, the epitome of unpretentiousness, was alive, humility was alive.

Extreme humility and self-denigration, that is, a person focusing only on his or her bad qualities, can cause depression and is bad. We need to learn to serve God out of joy. One of the curses mentioned in the Torah[86] comes as a result of not serving God with a happy heart.

Matzah has been proposed as one of the symbols of humility. Although it is made with the same ingredients as bread, it is much

[84] Samuel 1 13:1-10 also Samuel 1 15:8-20
[85] Sotah 49a.
[86] Deuteronomy 28:47.

denser and takes up only a fraction of the volume of bread with the same weight. Leaven represents a lie. It is puffed up and assumes a different shape, fooling a person as to its true ingredients. So too, proud people swell up with their own sense of importance and persuade themselves that they are better than they really are. A humble person can be compared to matzah, having no stuffy pomposity. I am what I am, plain and simple.

The Antidote

The Mishnah in Pirke Avot (3:1) gives us a remedy for the three destructive motivators of jealousy, lust and ego. It tells us to:

"Remember three things and you will never sin:

"Where did you came from - a putrid drop." This thought helps to counteract pride. Just thinking about our most humble origins should give us humility.

"Where are you going to - a place of dust and worms." This thought should help us to counteract our desires. After all, if we cannot take anything with us, why do we desire it?

"In front of whom you will give judgment - in front of the King of Kings, the Holy One Blessed be He." This thought counteracts feelings of jealousy, for if we would only realize that there is a God, who sustains each person according to his or her needs, we would never be jealous.

Equilibrium, - The Golden Mean

Equilibrium in life is essential.[87] Just as a person should not engage in excesses of desire, Judaism does not approve

---

[87] Rambam Hilkhot De'ot 1:2-3.

of a monastic lifestyle. We are to partake of and enjoy, in moderation the pleasurable things that God created.

There is a famous dictum in the Jerusalem Talmud.[88] Rabbi Chizkiyah said, in the name of Rav, that God will judge a person for seeing new fruit and not partaking of it. Rabbi Elazar was so concerned about this statement that he would save up money in order to purchase and eat from all new fruits during the year.

The Torah[89] discusses the laws of a Nazirite. A Nazirite is a person who took a vow to become a Nazir and has to keep the following additional laws:

a) He has to grow his hair, and is not allowed to shave or cut his hair.
b) He is not allowed to drink wine or partake of any grape product.
c) He is not allowed to defile himself by coming in contact with dead bodies, including even those of his own relatives.

Rabbi Eliezer Hakappar[90] asks why the Nazirite had to bring a sin offering after the end of the period of his vow. His answer is similar to the dictum in the Jerusalem Talmud above: He had afflicted himself by abstaining from wine. Rabbi Eliezer continues, if a person who only deprived himself of wine and thus afflicted himself is called a sinner, how much more so a person sins when he afflicts himself by depriving himself of other permissible pleasures.

A Person's Traits Are Consistent with Their Personality

A person is always consistent. There is no such thing as acting uncharacteristically. "I just wasn't myself," in fact means "I was

[88] Yerushalmi, end of the fourth chapter of Kiddushin.
[89] Numbers 6.
[90] Nazir 19a, quoted by Rashi Numbers 6:11.

myself; I simply may not have been aware that this potential was in me." A bit of what one truly is emerges in everything that a person does. The ways we talk, the ways we act are aspects of our deepest selves that intrude on everything we do. Our spontaneous actions often reflect our character and subconscious thoughts.

This point may be illustrated by the following story. It is said that when a certain rabbi wanted to know how his son, who was studying at an out-of-town Yeshivah, was doing, he traveled to the Yeshivah and went to see the boy's room. When he saw that his son's bed and closet were very neat and tidy, he was satisfied with the knowledge that his son was learning well. He did not need any reports from the teachers. An orderly mind is able to discriminate well in learning and to absorb well, while a disorderly mind cannot.

As an illustration of this principle, let us take a hypothetical example, an incident whereby a person who slandered another was subsequently ordered to kill him. He hesitated. The slandered person was, after all, a great human being. However, the king who was ordering the execution knew our principle well. If you've already slandered him, you'll kill him. It's part of your character and your relationship with this person. Slander lies on a continuum where murder can be found down the line.[91]

Naturally, this would have significant impact on the process of repentance, or re-aligning one's self to the directives of the Torah. There is no excuse. A person cannot say that "it was not the real me." Only by altering one's behavior, and through meaningful prayer, can one modify who one truly is.

Minor Personality Problems

People should not discount the minor faults or strengths of their personality as being insignificant, for it is the small parts

---

[91] Samuel 1. 22:22.

**that add up to the whole. A malfunction in one seemingly
minor area can cause disturbances throughout the system.**

Take the example of the human body. If a small organ does not
work properly, the whole body will be affected. This is stressed
in the blessing that should be recited upon relieving oneself. If an
orifice that should be open is blocked or if a valve that should be
closed opens, we would be unable to exist.

Another example is a car engine or any other type of complex
machinery. Sometimes a small inexpensive part can prevent
the whole engine from working properly. Another example
is a complex computer system, where a small flaw in the most
powerful and complex system can sometimes bring everything
crashing down.

A minor fault in the earth's crust can sometimes cause major
earthquakes. A crack in the foundations in a mighty edifice can
sometimes bring the whole edifice crashing down; so too with the
human personality. Sometimes a small fault can cause a major
repercussion and leave lasting damage.

This concept of small things leaving major effects is alluded to at
the beginning of the Torah portion of Mishpatim (Exodus 21:1).
Much comment has been elicited by a single letter at the beginning
of the portion, the opening "vav" of "AND these are the statutes
that you shall place before them." At first glance it would seem
hard to find a greater contrast than between the magnificent awe-
inspiring revelation at Mount Sinai and the continuation into the
seemingly petty mundane laws that follow: pertaining to the family
life of a slave, to assorted forms of homicide, torts and bailments,
to judicial proceedings, agriculture, lost items, and more. The
conjunctive 'vav' ('and'), connecting these two portrayals of
Jewish religious experience, highlights the contrast between them,
while binding them together as consecutive points on a spiritual

continuum. All areas of life are intertwined, and holiness derives from halachically-correct business dealings no less than from piety in matters of ritual.

Immediately after the recognition of God's power, through the miracles of the plagues and the splitting of the sea, and the revelation at Sinai, the Torah commences with these mundane laws because they are as much an expression of God's greatness as the great revelations. Small things count. They add up.

Quick Fixes

Elijah the Prophet was living at a reasonably successful time in the history of the Northern Kingdom of Israel, at least materially, but spiritually it was a disaster. Omri, the previous King, had done well in battle and had left the kingdom a safer place. His son Ahab was also a great warrior and diplomat. Unfortunately he had married Jezebel, an idolatrous princess from the neighboring kingdom of Tyre. Jezebel brought with her four hundred prophets of 'baal zebub' (lord of the flies, a pagan idolatry) and one hundred prophets of Ashtarte (god of the trees) and instituted these strange forms of worship in Israel.

Elijah had announced to the King that because of his sanction of these evil acts there would be a drought. The drought was extremely severe, just as the prophet had predicted. The King was personally involved with the search for new water supplies. He met with the prophet Elijah[92] and blamed him for the sorry state of affairs. Elijah told him that, on the contrary, the drought was caused because the king had condoned idolatry. Elijah then challenged the so-called prophets of the Baal to a spiritual duel on Mount Carmel (now a part of Haifa in Israel).

---

[92] I Kings 18:17.

King Ahab gathered the people to Mount Carmel and brought the prophets of Baal to bring a sacrifice of an ox to their god. Elijah told the people that the god who would send fire from heaven to devour the sacrifice would be acclaimed as the true God. The false prophets tried their best, pleading and crying to their god to send fire to devour their offering, but nothing happened. Elijah started mocking their god. "Maybe he is asleep. Maybe he went to relieve himself..." he scoffed. Finally they gave up and left in disgrace.

Elijah built an altar to God and had a trench dug around it. He placed the pieces of the sacrifice on it and prayed to God to perform a miracle and send fire to consume his sacrifice. This took place and the people shouted twice "Ado-nai is the Lord!" They had finally witnessed a tremendous miracle that could not be rationalized. At Elijah's bidding, they hunted down the false prophets of Baal and had them killed. When Queen Jezebel heard of these events, she became furious and threatened Elijah with death.

Even though he had just performed an amazing miracle in front of all the people and they had acknowledged God, nobody lifted a finger to save him from being killed by the evil Queen Jezebel. Massive miracles don't seem to change people over the long term.

A similar idea is expressed in the revelation of God to Elijah in I Kings 19:11. Elijah saw massive powerful winds, but God was not in the wind. He felt a tremendous earthquake, but God was not in the earthquake. After the earthquake came a terrifying fire, but God was not in the fire. After the fire Elijah heard a calm, soft voice. When Elijah heard this voice, he went out and stood by the entrance of the cave and the voice spoke to him. I think that this was a lesson for Elijah in particular, and to anyone else who has the good fortune to read or hear about this event.

God was teaching him that you cannot create lasting change in people by performing great and awesome miracles. It is the

small and mundane acts represented by the calm, quiet voice that are more effective in having a lasting effect. Artificial highs can be great while they last, but the consequence is that a person comes crashing down the day after.

The Talmud,[93] during the time of the Roman persecution of the Jews, cites a debate about Jewish survival. The Rabbis of the time were worried that with Torah scholars being murdered, the Torah would be forgotten. Rabbi Chaninah boasted that since he was still alive, there was no fear of this happening, for with his tremendous intellect and memory he would single-handedly restore the Torah to its former glory.

The Talmud goes on to relate that Rabbi Chiya took parchment and wrote the Five Books of the Bible on five scrolls. He took five boys and taught each one a book. Then he made each one of them teach his book to the others. He then wrote the six orders of the Mishnah on six scrolls and taught them separately to six boys. He then made them teach each other the Mishnah that they had learned. Rabbi Judah the Prince, the editor of the Mishnah, commented, "How great are the deeds of Rabbi Chiya." He preserved the Torah. This story also emphasizes that it is not through a single great event or person that spirituality will be preserved, but through small mundane actions, like teaching Torah to a child.

Elijah the prophet thought that he could alter the people's belief with a single act of revelation. He was tremendously depressed that this did not work. Moses, with all the ten plagues, revelation, wonders and miracles could not alter the way his followers thought. The whole generation was condemned by God to die in the wilderness. No quick fixes were possible.

Many people today are looking for quick fixes, for quick artificial spiritual highs. They search for them in different cults or they try

---

[93] Ketubot 103b.

alcohol or drugs. The effects are potent, but they come crashing down soon afterward. The Torah frowns on artificial highs, especially in the service of God.[94] The same is true in personality change. It is unhealthy to make dramatic radical changes that cannot last. Small, incremental, constructive changes that add up are better, and are not felt by those performing them to be a great burden.

Habit is The Key to Altering Personality

The Torah is a tremendous agent for behavior modification. Only now is modern psychology grappling with the effects that our actions have on our thought processes. Behavior modification predicts that a change in behavior can and will alter the way a person thinks. The opposite, however, may not be true. People who change the way they think may still not be able to change the way they act. The habits that they have created may be too ingrained.

Maimonides, the great philosopher, gives us an inkling of the power of habit. He writes[95] that after a person does a bad deed three times, he or she does it the fourth time without even thinking. Similarly, if a person does a good deed three times, it becomes second nature to him or her. The most effective way to break a bad habit is not to engage in it three times in a row, in order to create a 'counter-habit.'

We are influenced the most by what we do, by what we say, hear, eat, touch and see. By performing mitzvot, a person is altering his or her personality and consciousness until the effects reach into the deepest recesses of the subconscious. This is why, more than any other religion, Judaism is a religion of action. Action, and not thought, plays the dominant role in the formation of human character.

---

[94] Leviticus 10:9.
[95] Hilkhot De'ot 1:7.

Self-Sacrifice to Change

There is a glaring question that most people rarely consider. Why is Mount Sinai not considered holy to the Jewish people today? Not only is Mount Sinai not considered holy, but we don't even know exactly where it is. This is hardly the treatment that you would expect for such a site, the location of a colossal revelation that caused vast historical and moral changes. Shouldn't Mount Sinai be a national holy site, to which we should be obliged to go on frequent pilgrimages?

Instead, Mount Moriah (the Temple Mount) is considered sacred, and on it were built two of our former temples. We pray facing the site of the Holy of Holies on Mount Moriah and we are commanded in the Torah to visit the site three times a year. Why is Mount Sinai not treated at least equally?

The answer is that Mount Sinai was consecrated by God and not by the deeds of the people. God declared it to be holy only temporarily, whereas Mount Moriah was sanctified by the deeds of Abraham who was prepared, at immense personal sacrifice, to serve God. Holiness created externally by God wears off if man does not deserve. The holiness that is earned by the incremental spiritual climbing of man never departs from him.

This principle is used by the Sefat Emet, one of the commentators on the Torah to answer an interesting question.[96] We perform the ceremony of Havdalah (Separation) at the end of the Sabbath (Shabbat) to delineate and separate between the holiness of the Sabbath and the mundane weekday. The same ceremony is performed at the conclusion of the festivals, with the exception that the blessings on the candle and the sweet-smelling spices are not recited. Why is there no blessing on the spices after a festival? The Sefat Emet explains that the reason for smelling the spices

---

[96] Leviticus 22:32.

after Shabbat is to revive ourselves from the sadness of the extra sanctity[97] (soul) of the Sabbath departing; this reason does not apply after a festival. The extra sanctity left over after a festival does not depart. The Shabbat is sanctified automatically by God, since He refrained from creating on that day. The festivals, however, are sanctified by us as the months are announced by the Rabbinical court which thereby fixes the dates for the festivals. What we achieve through our own spiritual striving is ours because it leaves a lasting effect on us.[98]

This is also a lesson of Parashat Tetzaveh, which is one of only two Torah portions after the birth of Moses that does not mention his name (the other being Nitzavim). The Parasha deals with the construction of a sanctuary to serve as a focal point for God's presence. This teaches us that our focus for spirituality should be independent of any one person.

Similarly, the Ran[99] asks why Moses, a stutterer, was given the task of being the teacher of the Torah? He answers that if God would have given the Torah through a very eloquent orator, people might have accepted it because they were dazzled by the power of his oratory, and not because they were impressed with the intrinsic value of the Torah itself.

So too, regarding the character traits of a person. It is only by virtue of sacrifice and discipline that these traits will be perfected, and not by some mysterious external intervention.

Small increments of spiritual growth that we achieve through our own efforts are extremely worthwhile and leave lasting effects.

---

[97] Neshamah Yeterah.

[98] See Rashbam and Tosafot Pesahim 102b other reasons.

[99] Acronym for Rabbenu Nissim of Gerona, 1308-1376, author of important commentaries on the Talmud and the halachic compendium of Rabbi Isaac Alfasi. Ran also authored responsa and left a collection of sermons.

Chapter 5. Sin and Guilt

There are four types of mistakes or sins a person can make:

1. A sin by accident ('onness') is non-punishable. For example, someone trips involuntarily and falls against the incandescent light switch on Shabbat, causing the light to go on. In civil cases, however, a person is even held accountable for damage done in his or her sleep, which is totally accidental.

2. A sin done in a state of forgetfulness ('shogeg') is not serious, but subjects one to a fine. For example, a person either forgets that it is Shabbat and switches on an incandescent light bulb, or he or she forgets that this particular act is prohibited. In Temple (Bet Hamikdash) times, the penalty for this category of transgression was a sin-offering ('Chatat'). It is interesting that the Torah prescribes an offering for this type of sin, and there is no excuse for someone who forgets. The cost and trouble involved in bringing this offering would serve as a reminder to the person on future occasions. It is rather like a person being fined for a traffic violation, which serves as a reminder to be more careful in the future.

3. The third variety of transgression is more serious. It is a premeditated sin, for the sake of pleasure (avvon). For example, a person desires to eat and goes to a non-kosher restaurant to satisfy his or her appetite. This type of purposeful sin was done by a person only to satiate some desire.

4. The last level is the worst: A sin for no reason other than to anger God ('pesha'). For example, a person who goes out of his or her way to eat, specifically, non-kosher food on Yom Kippur,[100] to show his or her utter contempt for the commandments (mitzvot).

---

[100] The Day of Atonement is a day spent on introspection when eating and drinking are prohibited unless a person has major health problems.

Dr. Abraham J. Twersky points out that modern psychology has placed great emphasis on guilt as a negative emotion, and that guilt should be eliminated, lest it hinder a person's creativity or cause a depressed mood. The implication is that people should not feel guilty. This attitude has resulted in some psychologists referring to Yom Kippur as being a preoccupation with guilt, and to Judaism as being obsessed with guilt.

He posits that this attitude is based on ignorance of both psychology and Judaism. Guilt is to the soul what pain is to the body. It is physical pain that alerts a person to something that is injurious to one's life and health, and it is spiritual pain (guilt) that alerts a person to something that is injurious to the soul.

There are some people with Syringomyelia, a disease of the spinal cord that destroys the nerve fibers that conduct the sensation of pain. Their nervous system does not function properly and they do not feel any pain. These people must be extremely careful that they don't do themselves serious injury, because they do not feel any pain. They can sustain severe burns, cuts or fractures without their body alerting them that they have been injured. This generally makes the injury worse, possibly even deadly, because the absence of feedback (pain) from their body prevents them from reacting appropriately. Pain is necessary because it warns us that something is wrong, very much like the warning lights on cars, which warn the driver that some mechanical part needs attention. Similarly guilt is the spiritual pain that warns us that something ethereal is going wrong.

The Functions of Guilt

1. Guilt is the spiritual pain that warns us that something is wrong.

2. Guilt is the primary deterrent from following powerful temptations. We generally avoid these temptations because we do not wish to suffer the distress of guilt or pangs of conscience.

3. Guilt causes us to apologize to someone whom we have offended and stimulates us to make amends whenever possible.

4. Guilt causes us to analyze our behavior and eliminate the actions that have caused us distress.

It is of course possible for guilt to be a sickness, if it occurs in the absence of any wrongdoing. This type of guilt requires treatment just as would physical pain with no disorder. Yes, Judaism is concerned with guilt, its alleviation.

We all have a conscience, called in traditional jargon the 'yetzer hatov.' Some of us utilize it as a valuable tool and sensitize ourselves to it. Others do not pay attention to the voice of their conscience and ignore it. They tell the conscience to go back to sleep. Rambam,[101] in explaining the mitzvah of blowing the shofar on Rosh Hashanah, states that its purpose is to awaken the conscience within us.

When a person in physical pain does not obtain medical help his or her condition may deteriorate drastically, similarly, if a person ignores spiritual pain, serious damage could occur to his or her spiritual well-being. Many people are adept at tranquilizing their feelings of guilt. For this they ultimately may bear a heavy price, 'karet', the excision of the soul.

---

[101] Hilkhot Teshuvah 3:4.

Notes

Chapter 6. Accountability

Awareness of Divine Providence

The first mitzvah[102] listed by Rambam in his book of commandments, entitled <u>Sefer Hamitzvot,</u> is the mitzvah to believe in God. This is the first of the 'ten commandments.' We are commanded to believe that there is a God who is both the Creator and is aware of and in control of what goes on. This is what we say in the Shema every day, 'The Lord (i.e. the Creator) is our God.' He is a personal God and has the ability to directly intervene and control any part of creation at any time. This concept is also the reason behind our frequent repetition that God freed us from slavery in Egypt. This reminds us that God has the power, if He wants to intervene in human events.

We believe that God is aware of our actions and what is going on around us twenty-four hours a day. In Deuteronomy 11:12 the Torah discusses Divine providence in the land of Israel. "The eyes of the Lord your God are on it from the beginning of the year to the end of the year."

Jonah tried running away from God and the Land of Israel thinking that Divine providence and prophecy do not extend to outside Israel. Imagine his surprise on discovering that God is knowable even in a fish in the depths of the ocean.

The Torah tells us in Devarim 4: "You who cling to Hashem your God you are all alive today." We learn from this that the secret of spiritual life is clinging to God.

Rambam[103] stated that depending on a person's closeness or distance from God is the level of Divine providence that Hashem

---

[102] A mitzvah is a commandment, not a good deed or suggestion.
[103] Moreh Nevuchim Part 3, chapter 18.

extends to a person. Rambam[104] has a great section that deals with our relationship with God. I am paraphrasing:

The intellect which emanates from God to us is the link that joins us to God. You have the power and the free choice to strengthen the bond, or weaken it, even break it entirely. The bond becomes stronger the more you direct your mind to God and seek His love. It will be weakened when you direct your mind to other things.

Even if you were the wisest person in respect to knowledge of God when you entirely turn your thoughts to necessary food or necessary business, you are not then with God and He is not with you, for the relationship between you is interrupted at these moments.

Plugging Into Your Energy Source

All creatures and gas or electric or electronic equipment need an energy source to live or work.

Humans obtain physical energy from food, machines from electricity or gas or other energy supply. Electric devices needs to be plugged in to a battery or the grid to operate hence the tremendous amount of research into battery technology to extend battery life and reduce charging times.

We humans don't realize that our souls, our spiritual life force, also require to be recharged. This spiritual recharging usually takes place in the morning when we awaken, then we thank God for restoring our pure soul and for giving strength to the weak. However there is a higher level a human can reach - to be connected to our CREATOR our Life Source throughout the day.

---

[104] The Guide For the Perplexed Section 3, Chapter 51.

This is alluded to in Deuteronomy 4:4: 'But you who **cling to Hashem, your God** - you are all alive today.'

The real Hebrew word for life is 'chai' the numerical value of which is 18 which is why it is popular to donate money in multiples of 18. However when referring to life it is usual to use the plural 'chayim' the numerical value of which is 68. (This is the numerical value of three powerful names of God.) The plural form is used because, although we don't realize it **we are all alive on two planes the physical and spiritual.** Our souls are recharged by plugging in to God, or clinging to Him which is the terminology used in the Torah.

A person involved with God receives a higher level of Divine protection and providence[105] then someone who is not that involved with God.

Many verses in the Torah command us to cling to God and develop a relationship with Him.

a) Deuteronomy 10:20 "You shall fear the LORD your God; you shall serve Him and **cling to Him**, and you shall swear by His name.
b) Deuteronomy 13:4 "You shall follow the LORD your God and fear Him; and you shall keep His commandments, listen to His voice, serve Him, and **cling to Him**.
c) Joshua 23:8 "But you are to **cling to the LORD your God**, as you have done to this day."
d) Deuteronomy 11:22 "For if you are careful to keep all this commandment which I am commanding you to do, to love the **LORD your God, to walk in all His ways and cling to Him**."
e) 2 Kings 18:6 '**For he clung to the LORD**; he did not depart from following Him, but kept His commandments, which the LORD had commanded Moses.'

---

[105] Hashgacha Pratit.

f)   Psalms 63:8 '**My soul clings to You**; Your right hand upholds me.'

g)   Jeremiah 13:11 **'For as the waistband clings to the waist of a man, so I made the whole household of Israel and the whole household of Judah cling to Me,'** declares the LORD, 'that they might be for Me a people, for renown, for praise and for glory...'

Many of our great personalities had very close relationships with God and this tremendously enhanced their greatness.

a)   God said to Abraham in Bereshit 14:1 I am your shield.[106]

b)   God said to Yitzchak "I will be with you and I will bless you".[107]

c)   God said to Yaakov "I am with you and will keep you".[108]

d)   God said to Moshe "Certainly I will be with you and this shall be a sign to you".[109]

e)   God said to Yehoshua "As I was with Moshe so I will be with you".[110]

A person connects with God by:

a)   performing mitzvot,

b)   praying,

c)   learning torah,

d)   saying berachot,

e)   thinking of God's holy name: King David stated[111], "I have set YHVH before me at all times. Given that the Torah forbids imagining any shape or image of God the only method we have of closely meditating on God is His holy name:

---

[106] This became the end of the first blessing in the amidah.

[107] Bereshit 26:3.

[108] Bereshit 28:15.

[109] Shemot 3:12.

[110] Yehoshua 1:5.

[111] Psalm 16:8.

The Talmud[112] stated that Rav Yaakov Bar Idi pointed out a contradiction: On the one hand the Torah states[113] God told Yaakov "I am with you and will guard you wherever you go". On the other hand it says[114] when Yaakov was told that Esav was coming with four hundred men Yaakov became very scared. Rav Yaakov Bar Idi answered that Yaakov was afraid that maybe he had committed a sin that caused him to lose Divine protection.

There are many beautiful psalms in Tehillim where King David cried out to God for protection. Among them are some that especially stand out. The world renowned Psalm 23 "Even though I walk through the valley of the shadow of death; I will fear no evil for You are with me; Your rod and staff comfort me…. Psalm 27, where King David thanked God from saving him from Goliath.[115] Psalm 42 when King David was hiding in a cave from King Saul and his men; who were hunting him.

The Mishnah,[116] expanded on the theme of awareness of God: 'Rebbi[117] says, remember three things and you will never sin... an eye that sees, an ear that hears, and all one's deeds are written down.' Everything is known before God, as we say in the Yom Kippur prayers, "You see kidneys and heart. Nothing is hidden from You." A person would never sin if they truly believed in, and continuously reflected on, God's providence.

There is a well-known story of a rabbi who was given a ride by a peddler in a wagon pulled by a horse. After a while, the horse was getting hungry. When they passed a field with an abundance of hay, the peddler got down from the wagon and told the rabbi to

---

[112] Brachot 4a.
[113] Bereshit 28:15.
[114] Bereshit 32:8.
[115] Ashkenazim add this psalm to their prayers the forty days between Rosh Chodesh Elul and Yom Kippur and some continue until Shemini Atzeret.
[116] Pirke Avot, Chapter 2, Mishnah 1.
[117] Rabbi Judah the Prince of Israel, middle first and second century sage and editor of the entire Mishnah.

keep a look out while he went to gather some hay for his horse. As soon as he arrived in the field to pick up the hay, the rabbi startled him with a shout, "Come back quickly! Someone is watching!" The peddler beat a hasty retreat. Empty-handed, he jumped onto the cart, and with a snap of the reins, galloped off. After a while, the peddler looked around him and slowed down. "Who was watching, rabbi?" he asked, "I don't see anyone!" The rabbi answered with perfect composure, "God was watching."

We have to ask ourselves, "Would we speed if we knew that there was a police car right behind us?" How can we disobey God's commands if we believe that He is watching?

Rationalization

If we know that God is watching, how can we do anything wrong?

The Talmud[118], made an interesting observation: 'A person does not sin unless a spirit of craziness enters him.' The Talmud is referring to the fact that a person, in order to sin, has to either forget that God is aware of what is going on at that instant, or to rationalize and persuade him or herself that the sin is permitted, that it doesn't matter, or it has no negative impact, etc. It is these thoughts of rationalizing a potentially evil act to which the Talmud refers as 'a spirit of craziness.'

The story of Adam and Eve in the Garden of Eden seems to be a simplistic one, but like various other stories in the Torah it can be understood on a multitude of different levels.[119] Some of the

---

[118] Sotah 3a.

[119] The sages of blessed memory in the Midrash Rabbah, Bemidbar 13, inform us that the Torah can be viewed and interpreted from seventy different perspectives. Just as white light, which appears to the viewer to be monochromatic can be split into its component parts when passed through a prism, so too the Midrashic elements of the Torah can be viewed from different perspectives and perceived differently, and yet remain within one tradition. Learning Torah has also been compared to peeling an onion. Whenever a layer is peeled, there is always another layer underneath. From the following story we can

classic biblical commentators were perplexed by the account of the 'serpent' in the story of Adam and Eve. Who or what was this serpent?

Rabbi Saadya Gaon (9th century Babylonian sage and Rosh Yeshivah), as quoted by Ibn Ezra, Genesis 3:1, makes the following observation: "We have never come across a snake that walks and talks!" He therefore explained that this was not a real snake but a veiled reference to the angel Samael, also called the Angel of Death (Malach Hamavet).

The Talmud[120] equated the following three entities: The Angel of Death; Satan (the prosecutor on high) and evil inclination (yetzer hara). According to this equation, what Rabbi Saadya Gaon seems to be saying is that the snake was none other than Eve's (Chava's) evil inclination.

Rabbi Ovadia Seporno,[121] on Genesis 3:1 further elucidates this theme. He states that the snake was Eve's imagination. The word for snake in Hebrew is 'nachash' and the word for 'to guess' or 'to imagine' is 'lenachesh'. He equates these two concepts. The snake within, or the evil inclination (yetzer hara), works through the imagination, which is triggered by what a person sees and thinks. According to these commentaries, the Torah is basically recording an internal debate that Eve had within herself, a conversation with her subconscious desires. We all converse with our subconscious desires every day, many times over. According to these commentaries, the Torah account of Eve's sin goes as follows:

---

comprehend the vastness of Torah learning. When Rabbi Eliezer Ben Hurkenus, (1st century CE) one of the leading sages of his time, was dying, the Talmud in Sanhedrin 68a states that he told his students that even though he was one of the great scholars of his generation (see Pirke Avot 2:8), he had gathered as much Torah learning from his Rabbis as a dog could lick water from the sea.

[120] Baba Batra 16a.

[121] Medieval Spanish rabbi, philosopher and bible commentator.

Her subconscious (snake within) to Eve seemingly-innocuously: "Did God tell you not to eat from any tree in the garden?" "We are allowed to eat from the trees in the garden, but from the tree located in the midst of the garden, God said not to eat and not to touch, lest we die!", she answered. The serpent (her subconscious) replied: "You will not die because God knows that on the day that you eat from it, your eyes will open and you will be like God, knowing good and evil." If we take this to be a conversation she had with her own subconscious desires or yetzer hara, this is a classic example of human rationalization. The stages used in her process of rationalization were:

(a) Pondering the mitzvah.

(b) Making mistakes in the actual command. God did not command Adam and Eve to abstain from touching the tree, only to refrain from eating its fruit. The commentaries tell us that Adam had invented this law to ensure that they would be further removed from the sin. This was the first man-made decree (gezerah), to prevent a person from sinning.

(c) Attributing false, selfish motives to God Himself. In this case the snake implied that this command of not eating the fruit was given to prevent human enhancement to God's level.

The narrative continues:

The woman saw that the tree was good for food, and it was desirous for the eyes and it was good for the intelligence, so she took from its fruit and ate, and she also gave to her husband with her and he ate.

Once she had rationalized her decision mentally, now came the clinching arguments, physical and intellectual attraction.

These desires are always at the back of our minds and urge us to rationalize so that they may be satisfied.

The human propensity for rationalization is enormous. We can rationalize anything.

According to Rabbi Ovadia Seporno, Eve really deluded herself into eating from the Tree of Knowledge. She also persuaded herself and her husband that only good results would flow from her actions. This was the prototype of all future sin.

When God later asked Adam (Bereshit 3:12) if he had eaten from the fruit, Adam passed the buck back to God by replying, "The woman you gave me, gave me from the tree." The audacity of Adam, in essence blaming God for his own mistake, also shows his power of rationalizing.

President Harry Truman used to have a sign behind his desk: 'The buck stops here.' Only we are responsible for our own actions.

Accepting Responsibility for our Actions

Our tendency to rationalize, and in essence beguile ourselves, is the reason behind the commandment in the third paragraph of the Shema: 'Do not follow after your heart and your eyes' ('Lo taturu acharei levavchem ve acharei enechem').

The human senses are likened to spies.[122] They constantly feed information to the brain. This is the reason that the last paragraph

---

[122] Although the third paragraph of the Shema precedes the previous two parshiot in the Torah, it is placed last in order of importance. The Talmud in Berachot discusses the reason for this. The first paragraph of the Shema deals with accepting the yoke of God's authority ('ol malchut Shamayim'). The second paragraph is where we accept the commandments. The last paragraph is where we refer to the power of the evil inclination, when God warns us not to go after the heart and eyes.

of the Shema is in the same Torah portion of Shelach[123] as that of the twelve spies that Moses had sent to spy out the land of Israel. The mistake of the ten spies also followed a pattern of rationalization, equating what they saw with what they desired.

> But the men who went up...said, "We are not able to go up against the people, for they are stronger than we." And they brought up an evil report of the land which they had spied to the people of Israel, saying, "The land, through which we have gone to spy, is a land that eats up its inhabitants; and all the people that we saw in it are men of a great stature. And there we saw the Nefilim, the sons of Anak, who come from the Nefilim; and we were in our own sight as grasshoppers, and so were we in their sight."

Their rationalization is most evident in the last line, where they claimed that they were like grasshoppers in the eyes of the Nefilim. How did they know how others viewed them? They rationalized.

There is a famous question on the verse in the Shema that instructs us not to follow our heart and our eyes. Why is the heart placed before the eyes? Normally the opposite sequence is true?

The answer: We cannot be blamed for the first things we see. After all, we do have to look around to avoid danger and to determine directions. Because this cannot be helped, we are not held accountable for the first glimpse. However, it is when we take the second glance following the suggestion or rationalizing of the mind that instructs the person to look at it some more, or in extreme cases to take it, is when we get into trouble.

This is why the verse in the Shema puts the heart before the eyes, because the first sight is usually innocent of any bad motive and therefore one is not accountable for it.

---

123   Numbers, Chapter 13:31.

Ben Ish Chai[124] has an interesting insight into the layout of a person's features. He posits that they are placed in order of importance. The mouth, i.e. taste, is the lowest of the senses as it has the lowest impact on our behavior and spirituality. Next is the nose, associated with the sense of smell, then the ears, associated with hearing. We are influenced a lot by what we hear, but the greatest influence on a person comes from sight. Above the eyes is the brain which is the final arbiter that receives and processes information from the senses and decides on a course of action.

If we examine the order of the blessings in the Havdalah prayer, said over a cup of wine at the end of Shabbat, thanking God for separating the holy from the profane, we find that the same order is used. First we say the blessing over wine, representing the mouth or the sense of taste; then the blessing over fragrance, representing the sense of smell. All the while, our ears are listening to these blessings, representing the sense of hearing then the blessing over light, alluding to the sense of sight, and finally the blessing of separation (Havdalah), thanking God for giving us the ability to distinguish between the Shabbat and the weekday, the holy and the profane, etc. This represents the brain, which should be the final arbiter between the senses and action.

Rambam (Yesodei Hatorah 4:7) explains that whenever the Torah refers to the heart as the seat of human emotion, it is really referring to the brain. Thus the Torah in the third paragraph of the Shema is

---

[124] Rabbi Joseph Haim was born in Baghdad, in 1835, and studied under Rabbi Abdullah Someich. He never served as official rabbi of Baghdad, although he was a popular preacher, and his sermons were attended by thousands of people. He wrote many works, of Halachah, Drashot and Kabbalah. One of these books, Ben Ish Chai, after which he was popularly known, is a brief summary of practical halachah (comparable to the Kitzur Shulchan Aruch) is very popular among Sephardic Jews to this day. Rabbi Joseph Haim also edited the text of the Sephardic prayer book, in which he included kabbalistic elements. His responsa include answers to queries from Baghdad, Iraq, and from all over the Far East: India, Singapore, Ceylon, Kurdistan, and elsewhere. Accordingly, valuable historical and sociological information about these communities can be gleaned from his responsa. Rabbi Joseph Haim visited Israel, where he was received with great honor by the local rabbis. He died in 1909.

warning us not to be enticed by our senses and the rationalizations of our minds.

We have to be extremely selective as to what enters our brain through the five senses. The senses are the gates through which all influences enter our minds. What we see, hear, taste, smell and touch has tremendous persuasive powers. The Torah alludes to this in Deuteronomy 16:18:

> Judges and officers shall you appoint in all your gates, which the Lord your God gives you, throughout your tribes; and they shall judge the people with just judgment. You shall not pervert judgment; you shall not overly respect persons, nor take a bribe; for a bribe blinds the eyes of the wise, and perverts the words of the righteous. Justice, only justice shall you pursue, that you may live, and inherit the land which the Lord your God gives you.

These verses refer to setting up a justice system of courts and law-enforcement officials. It may also be alluding to the idea mentioned above that we should place judges and police at all our gates i.e. the gates of a person, which are the senses. We need to judge and police our senses to keep out any evil influence.

The Talmud[125] states that one of the qualifications for a judge to be a member of the Jewish high court (Sanhedrin) was the ability to prove logically that a non-kosher insect is kosher. The judge had to know the power of rationalization in order to qualify to sit on the bench. He would better be able to understand human nature in general, and would be a better judge of it. We all have this ability of being able to rationalize. It is part of the human psyche.

---

[125] Sanhedrin 17a.

Non-Accountability

The Talmud excludes three categories of human beings from accountability for their deeds:

a) Deaf-mutes. In times prior to Helen Keller, who was responsible in part for tremendous strides in education for the disabled, deaf-mutes unfortunately could not communicate at all. Since they could not be educated, the Talmud did not hold them accountable for their deeds.

b) Insane people, since they act irrationally, cannot be held accountable for their actions. The Talmud[126] lists three criteria to define an insane person: a person who travels alone at night (in dangerous places); a person who sleeps in a cemetery; a person who tears his or her own clothes. Rabbi Joseph Karo[127] states that, according to Rambam, these are just examples of symptoms. Obviously there are many other kinds of psychosis for which people may be categorized as not being in full control of themselves, and thus not accountable for their actions.

c) Children who are not yet Bar or Bat Mitzvah[128] are not liable for their actions. Parents are rabbinically commanded to educate and discipline their children. This idea is the source for the custom of the father of a Bar Mitzvah boy reciting a blessing thanking God for exempting him from culpability for the future transgressions of his son.

Ignorance and Forgetfulness

Unless there are extenuating circumstances, people are held liable for their actions. Obviously, people who know more and have had

[126] Chagiga 3b.
[127] Bet Yosef, Even Haezer, Chapter 121.
[128] Under age 12 for a girl and thirteen for a boy.

a better education have a greater degree of accountability than those who do not know as much. Ignorance by itself is no excuse, unless the person had no inkling that there is anything to learn. We Jews have been labeled the 'People of the Book.' Unfortunately, the vast majorities of Jews today are ignorant of its contents and are unaware of the tremendous amount of Jewish literature, probably hundreds of thousands of volumes on assorted Jewish subjects spanning three and a half millennia that are available. On the occasional attendance at synagogue services, the average Jew may come in contact with the bible and the prayer-book. In our generation, there is an excellent assortment of Jewish books available in English, and people should strive to read as much as possible about their heritage.

It is a biblical commandment for every Jew to write a Torah-scroll (Sefer-Torah). According to the famous medieval commentator Rabbenu Asher (Rosh), a person fulfills this obligation today by buying Hebrew books. This law is codified by the Code of Jewish Law.[129]

The Mishnah[130] deals with the level of culpability of various people. It discusses the topic of a person who breaks a Shabbat law unintentionally. An unintentional ('shogeg') prohibited act on Shabbat is committed through forgetfulness, either by forgetting that it was Shabbat or by forgetting that this particular act was forbidden. The Mishnah differentiates between three categories of people and their culpability:

1. The lowest level of culpability is that of a person who never knew anything about the concept of Shabbat. This person is described by the Talmud as a 'tinok shenishba,' a person who was captured as a baby and raised totally unaware of being Jewish. What is the culpability of this individual upon

---

[129] Yoreh Deah 270:2.
[130] Chapter 7 of Tractate (Masechet) Shabbat.

realizing that he or she is a Jew? The person has to bring one sin offering for breaking all the Sabbaths (Shabbatot) during his or her lifetime up till that point. It is only considered one case of forgetfulness, since he or she was unaware of the whole concept of Shabbat.

2. The second level in the order of culpability is of a person who was aware of the concept of Shabbat, but was unaware of the minutiae of the laws. This person is liable to bring one unintentional sin offering for every single Shabbat that was not observed in all its Biblical laws. It is regarded as though he forgot every single Shabbat, but since he didn't know the laws, he is not culpable for them at all.

3. The third level is that of a person who knew the concept of Shabbat and all the laws of Shabbat, and forgot the laws. He has to bring a sin offering for every single one of the laws that he forgot.

The ability to bring a sin offering was limited to those who broke laws unintentionally. Those who broke laws intentionally, without witnesses, had no recourse except through repentance (teshuvah), which we will discuss in a later chapter.

It is fascinating that forgetfulness of the law was not considered a valid excuse. The concept is that people do not forget things that are important to them. An individual who forgets something demonstrates that this matter is not important to him or her. A man who forgets his wife's birthday or their wedding anniversary would not be looked at in a favorable light. A child who forgot to do his homework would not be easily excused by his teacher.

We are to be continually mindful of who we are and what our responsibilities are.

Judgment (Din and Cheshbon)

When a person invests money in an interest-bearing account, he or she receives back the capital invested, plus the interest on the capital. So too, when a person performs a meritorious act, he or she is judged favorably and is rewarded for the deed itself.

1. This primary act of judgment is called 'din' in Hebrew.

2. The additional good deeds that may accrue as a result of the original deed are also judged favorably and are rewarded. The act of judgment on the secondary effects of the original deed is called 'Cheshbon' in Hebrew. Since the effects of the deed may vary over time and are usually compounded, a person's soul is judged even after death. This is the reason why we pray for the deceased many years after they passed away.

Take the fortunate example of a generous individual who made a contribution to a Talmudical college (yeshivah). The 'din' is the favorable judgment received for the first act of giving. Let us say that, because of his or her donation, the yeshivah was able to train twenty rabbis and they in turn eventually open their own Yeshivot and successively produce twenty rabbis each. The magnanimous individual is rewarded for the secondary results of his original deed 'Cheshbon'. Each of the rabbis is another tremendous merit for this philanthropic individual.

This beneficent person will be judged as having performed a righteous act of charity (tzedakah). Then he or she will earn the interest payments, a percentage of all the good deeds and learning through the generations that are attributable to his first act.

We have to realize that when we perform a good deed it is not just a one-time event that is only rewarded once, but we also get credit for all the effects of that deed. This is comparable to when a person throws a stone into a pool of water. It causes a splash that is followed by ripples, just as the person was directly responsible for the first splash, so too he or she is responsible for the ripples. The splash is analogous to the direct judgment or reward for the action itself (the 'din'), and the ripples are analogous to the reward or punishment for the outcomes directly or even indirectly attributable to that action (the 'Cheshbon').

'Din' and 'Cheshbon' also apply in the case of demerits like that of Cain and Abel. Cain killed his brother Abel. The 'din', immediate judgment, was that Cain as a murderer was liable for the death of one human being. *Cheshbon* calculates the ripple effect of the deed. Cain, unless his repentance was accepted, was not only judged for killing Abel, but was also judged for preventing countless other generations, the future progeny of Abel, from being born.

Meditate on the Consequences of One's Actions

Sometimes, a person may do a good deed where the primary judgment (din) is good, but where the secondary judgment on the results and outcomes ('Cheshbon') of the deed are bad. Other times, a person may do bad deeds where the immediate judgment (din) may be bad, but where the outcome ('Cheshbon') is favorable.

A mitzvah is a command. We have to obey it unless there are extenuating circumstances, as in the case of saving a life.[131] However, when it comes to going above and beyond the basic

---

[131] Pikuach nefesh - saving a life generally takes priority over all the other commandments, based on the verse in Leviticus 18:5 '...and live by them (the mitzvot).' All the commandments of the Torah are set aside in deference to 'pikuah nefesh,' except the three cardinal sins of murder, idolatry and adultery. See Rambam Hilkhot Yesodei Hatorah, Chapter 5:2, for further clarification. According to Rambam, if a person gave his life to fulfill another mitzvah, apart from the three cardinal sins, he is held accountable for committing suicide. See Yoma 85b and Tosafot Avodah Zarah 27b "Yakhol," who argues with Rambam that if a person wishes to die rather than transgress any mitzvah, it is to be considered a righteous act and not suicide. Life may not be shortened by any positive action, and extreme care is required, lest life be accidentally shortened.

mitzvah, we have to examine the extras carefully and farsightedly to see if the results will be good or bad.

Rabbi Moshe Haim Luzatto, in his famous ethical work Path of the Just, (Mesilat Yesharim), has a section called 'Weighing Piety'. In this section, he mentions this extremely important rule which we should all apply to the gray areas in our lives.

He gives as an example the case of a pious person who would run[132] to synagogue each day to pray. It was a very strange sight to witness this pious man running, and people would laugh and mock him when they saw him run by. On one hand, he performed the worthy act of running to synagogue, but on the other he caused others to mock him, and thus was guilty of placing a 'stumbling block before the blind.'[133]

Sometimes people try to do good by taking on themselves extra strictures (chumrot or hiddurim), that go far beyond the basic laws (halachah) without thinking of the consequences of their actions on themselves, their families, and on their surroundings. These extra strictures may then make them feel that Judaism is too much of a burden, and this may make them want to cut back on even essential mitzvot. So the result of their good deed may turn out to be bad.

This can be compared to a person buying a luxurious automobile on credit, but after ordering every imaginable accessory item he or she cannot keep up with the credit payments, and the car is repossessed.

---

[132] Running to synagogue is not a mitzvah, but an extra (hiddur) stricture, based on a verse in Psalms 55:15, 'To God's house we will go in haste.'

[133] The Torah (Leviticus 19:14) prohibits placing a stumbling block before the blind. Rashi explains this command (mitzvah) in two other ways, apart from its literal interpretation, which is also valid.

a) It is prohibited to give bad advice to someone who is unaware of the pitfalls involved.

b) It is forbidden to directly cause someone else to sin. (see Ramban, Bereshit 3:13).

Let us, for example, take a case where individuals take upon themselves an additional stricture not to eat in any kosher restaurant because they don't want to rely on any kosher supervision other than their own. According to Jewish law,[134] we may rely on the testimony of one 'reliable witness'[135] that a ritual was performed according to specifications. In the case of a restaurant under kosher supervision, one is permitted to rely on the veracity of a 'reliable supervisor' (mashgiach) that the kashrut is in order.

If this person usually works in or visits places where it is inconvenient to take prepared food from home, and therefore is used to eating out in kosher restaurants, the person may not be able to accept this additional burden and may abandon the dietary laws altogether.

Sometimes the evil inclination (yetzer hara) encourages us to become extra-pious in order to eventually break us.

Not to Add or Subtract a Mitzvah

The Torah[136] commands us not to add or subtract from the six hundred and thirteen commandments. The less-observant individual may be tempted to subtract from the commandments, but the Torah warns him or her not to. The more-observant individual may want to do the opposite and add to the commandments, so there is a special mitzvah warning that individual as well.

Rashi, on the Torah (Genesis 3:3), states that this was the mistake that Eve made. God had commanded her husband Adam not to eat from the tree of knowledge. Eve added to this command and told the serpent that God also commanded them not to touch the tree as well. Rashi says that the serpent pushed Eve into touching the

---

[134] Code of Jewish Law, Yoreh Deah 127:1.
[135] A male or female who is over Bar or Bat mitzvah age, who is known to be honest and fastidious in his or her observance of the commandments.
[136] Deuteronomy 13:1.

tree by accident and nothing happened, so she was persuaded that nothing would happen if she ate from its fruit either.[137]

Every day in the evening prayer, just before the Amidah (the silent standing prayer), we say the following words: "...and remove the Satan from in front of us and from behind us." The Satan in front of us can be understood as the inclination that blocks us from making any kind of spiritual progress, but what is the Satan behind us? The Satan behind us could be the inclination that is pushing us in the right direction, but with dizzying speed, with no time to think and meditate on the consequences of our actions, which may lead to a crash.

We have to examine not only our actions, but also their consequences.

---

[137] The Dubno Maggid gives a beautiful parable to elucidate why we should not add to God-given commandments:

A person was preparing to host a big reception in his house. Not having enough cups, he went to his neighbor next door to borrow some. The next day, along with the cups he had borrowed, he returned an additional small cup. When asked by his generous neighbor why he was giving an extra cup, the man gave the dubious response that the small cup was the baby of the big cups he had borrowed and he was thus returning the baby with its parents. The next day, once again in need of help, he went to his neighbor to borrow some plates. The neighbor willingly lent him the plates, which were duly returned with an extra small plate, with the same lame excuse that this was a baby of the large plates he had borrowed. It was graciously received by the generous neighbor. The next day the man came back to his neighbor's house, this time to borrow some large gold serving trays. The neighbor had no qualms about lending the trays. On the contrary, he was looking forward with great glee to the latest new arrival. Unfortunately, things did not work out as the neighbor had planned. The next day nothing was returned to him, no gold trays and no gold baby tray. After wistfully waiting for a few days, he went to claim his rightful property. "Oh my dear neighbor, I don't know how to break the bad news to you," the borrower sobbed, "I would have come earlier but I didn't want to ruin your day." "Why what is the matter?" was the startled reply. "Your beautiful gold trays, they died in childbirth!" "You crook!" shouted the generous neighbor, "You rotten thief! Everyone knows that trays can't have children." "Well," came the smooth response, "you didn't say that when I gave you the baby cup or the baby plate."

The point of the parable is that when we add to the mitzvot we somehow feel that we own them, which if true, allows us also to eventually subtract from them as well.

The Importance of Motivation

There is a discussion in the Talmud[138] as to the value of the motivation behind a deed. It discusses the famous ethical question of whether the ends justify the means.

> Ulla said "Tamar was immoral and Zimri was immoral. Tamar was immoral, and from her came Kings and Prophets. Zimri was immoral, and tens of thousands of Jews died as a result."

The difference between Tamar and Zimri was their motivation. Tamar had pure motives when she seduced Judah, (See Chapter 7 for a full discussion of Tamar's deed.). Her intention was to have a child to continue the name of her deceased husband (the mitzvah of Yibum). Zimri, a prince of the tribe of Simon during the forty years of wandering in the wilderness, on the other hand, was steeped in immorality, purely for his own base self-gratification.

This opinion in the Talmud implies that the reward and punishment for a deed depends on, among other things, the intentions behind it. Even bad deeds with good motives have value.

The Talmud continues,
> For the value of the forty-two sacrifices that the evil Balak made, he merited that Ruth would descend from him.

Balak was the King of Moab when the Israelites, after nearly forty years of wandering in the wilderness, came close to his land to go through to Israel. Worried that the Israelites would destroy him, and realizing that their power was spiritual from God, Balak hired Bilaam, a gentile prophet, to curse the Israelites. Balak offered up forty-two sacrifices to God at the behest of Bilaam, in order

---

[138] Nazir 23b.

to receive the necessary spiritual energy to curse the Israelites. Instead of cursing the Israelites Bilaam's prophecy came in the form of blessings. One of the verses of his blessings are even said on entering the synagogue every morning. "How goodly are your tents, O Jacob, your dwelling places, O Israel."[139]

Ironically, the sole purpose of Balak's sacrifices to God was to try and help Bilaam obtain the spiritual energy to curse the Jews. Even though his motives were improper, Balak did a good deed and was rewarded by having a close descendant who would convert to Judaism and be the forerunner of the Messianic line through King David. Balak even has the great honor of having a Torah portion (parashah) named after him, presumably for the same reason.

If We Only Knew How God Will Describe Our Deeds

The Midrash[140] quotes Rabbi Yitzchak, the son of Meryon, as stating the following:

> "When a person does a mitzvah, he should do it with a complete heart. If Reuben would have known that God would write his praises in the Torah, that he advised his brothers not to kill Joseph, but to place him in a pit, (his intention having been to save Joseph from the pit when the other brothers were not around),[141] Reuben would have carried Joseph back to his father on his own shoulders.

> Similarly, the Midrash continues, if Aaron, the brother of Moses, would have realized how God would refer to him in the Torah, he would have acted differently. In the story of the appearance of God to Moses at the burning bush,[142] God promised Moses that Aaron, his brother,

---

[139] Numbers 24:5.
[140] Midrash Rabbah, Ruth 5.
[141] Bereshit 37, 'And Reuben heard and saved him from their hands.'
[142] Exodus 4.

would come to greet him when Moses would return to Egypt. Had Aaron known that the details of his reception for Moses would be recorded for generations, he would have come to greet Moses in a festive and elaborate way, instead of with just a plain greeting.

The Midrash brings a third case, that of Boaz, who was a central figure in the story of Ruth. We know that Boaz was related to Ruth's deceased husband, Machlon. When Boaz heard that Ruth was gleaning the fallen stalks in his field,[143] Boaz invited her to partake of a meal of some roasted wheat. The Midrash comments that if Boaz would have known that the menu of what he gave Ruth to eat would be recorded for posterity, he would have offered her a much more elaborate meal of fatted calves, considered a delicacy in those days."

In these examples brought by the Midrash, Reuben, Aaron and Boaz all perform meritorious deeds, and yet, if they had known that these events would be recorded by God for posterity, they would have done them with much more enthusiasm and generosity.

We see from the Midrash that if we could only know what God thinks about us and our actions, even good ones, or if we would think our actions are being recorded somewhere for others to look at and examine, we would be many times more careful with what we do and how we do it.

The Torah places great emphasis on how Abraham, our forefather, performed the mitzvah of hospitality. It stresses that his guests were total strangers to him. It also emphasizes his magnanimous and enthusiastic behavior.[144]

---

[143] According to Torah law, if two stalks of grain fall from the reaper, they have to be left where they fell, set aside to be gleaned by the poor. This mitzvah of charity is called leket.

[144] Bereshit 18:2.

'He ran toward them from the entrance of the tent, and bowed to the ground. Then he said "My lords, if I find favor in your eyes, please pass not away from your servant. Let some water be brought and wash your feet, and recline beneath the tree. I will fetch a morsel of bread that you may sustain yourselves..." ...Abraham hastened to the tent to Sarah and said "Hurry!..Make cakes." Then Abraham ran to the cattle, took a calf, tender and good... He ran to greet them; he addressed them with immense honor, offering them hospitality.'

We see how Abraham performed the mitzvah of having guests with zest, enthusiasm and in an expeditious manner, despite his weakened post-circumcision state. His main concern was other people's welfare, not only his own. He is the role model we need to emulate. Shammai, in Pirke Avot 1:15, comments that we should say little and do a lot (to emulate Abraham).

As mentioned above, the Mishnah[145] compares the reward of a mitzvah to return on an investment of capital. The return consists of interest payments and capital payments. The Mishnah lists various mitzvot for which a person receives interest payments on the reward for that mitzvah in this world, and receives the capital of the reward for that mitzvah in the world to come: honoring one's parents; acts of kindness; hospitality; arising for prayers in the synagogue; making peace between people, including between husband and wife; and finally, learning Torah is equivalent to all the above combined.

It has been explained that the interest payments are not for the actual mitzvah, but for the way in which the mitzvah was performed. If the mitzvah was performed with extra devotion, enthusiasm, love, caring, and extra expense, a person receives additional reward in this world. Because of the extra devotion he applied to the mitzvot

---

[145] Peah 1:1.

he performed, the merits of Abraham for all are so great that they are still able to afford his descendants, protection in this world.

We also learn from a case involving Abraham the importance of pure motives. Abraham made war against four powerful Kings in order to save his brother-in-law and nephew, Lot, from their hands.[146] He was successful in battle and freed Lot and all the other captives, including the King of Sodom. The Torah then reports a conversation that Abraham had with the King of Sodom in which the King offered him all the spoils of war if he could keep all the people. Abraham refused to take anything, even though as victor he was entitled to everything. His reason was that the King of Sodom shouldn't be able to say that he made Abraham rich.

The commentaries ask why it is that Abraham took money and gifts from Pharaoh and Avimelech[147] when they had kidnapped and then freed his wife. Why didn't he refuse their offers of wealth with same explanation that he offered the King of Sodom? Wasn't he concerned that they would say that they had made him wealthy? One commentary answers that since Abraham had engaged in this war with the four kings to fulfill the mitzvah of redeeming captives, he refused any financial benefits resulting from his victory, which could detract from his pure motives.

What Goes Around Comes Around –
People's Actions Come Back to Haunt Them

We see from the story of how Jacob tricked his father Isaac and his brother Esau,[148] how the actions of people come back to haunt them later. He tricked his father by placing goat's skin on his arms and around his neck. Since Isaac was blind, he would mistakenly think that Jacob was his hairy brother Esau, his father's favorite

---

[146] Bereshit 14:21.
[147] Bereshit 12:16, 20:14.
[148] Bereshit 27:19.

son. The result of this trick was that he had to run away to escape his brother's wrath and leave his father for twenty-two years.

Jacob was forced into exile in perpetual fear of his brother Esau's revenge. He was compelled under humiliating circumstances to visit his uncle Laban in a penniless state, and to rely on his uncle's good will. Jacob was hired by his uncle Laban as a shepherd, a menial position for a millionaire's son who had never lifted a finger before.[149] Jacob agreed to work for his uncle for seven years to gain Laban's daughter Rachel's hand in marriage. After seven years of hard, exhausting work, the time came for his marriage to Rachel. However, the crafty Laban tricked his nephew and substituted Leah for Rachel.[150] When Jacob challenged his uncle, the response was tongue-in-cheek, and a slap in the face. "It is not done in our place to give the younger before the elder." Laban was alluding to his tricking of Esau, thus preventing Jacob from further protest. He was made to work an extra seven years for his beloved Rachel.

Laban changed Jacob's wages many times (Bereshit 31:7). When Jacob ran away, Laban chased him with a small army in order to kill him. Jacob was saved by God's intervention.
Later, after giving much of his hard-earned wealth to pacify his brother with gifts, he was understandably terrified when he heard that Esau was approaching, accompanied by four hundred men.

Finally, after pacifying his brother and his father-in-law, Jacob sought to retire in his ancestral land, free from all enemies and worries. Unfortunately, this was not to be. Immediately he was confronted with the troubles relating to his daughter Dinah, and then those surrounding his son Joseph.

---

[149] Bereshit 29:15.
[150] Bereshit 29:23.

The worst payback was when Jacob was tricked by his own sons. The comparison to his trickery is both ironic and poignant.[151] They dipped Joseph's beautiful coat into goat's blood and brought it back for their father to recognize. He was mistaken into believing that Joseph was killed by a wild beast and mourned for his lost son for twenty-two years.[152]

Judah, the brother who had advocated selling Joseph, was eventually forced to advocate his own slavery when he bargained with Joseph for the freedom of Benjamin.[153] The brothers, who had kept Joseph in terrible suspense when he was in the pit, while they sat down to have a meal, were also kept in suspense as to their own fate and the fate of Benjamin. Benjamin, the brother who had nothing to do with this transaction, was eventually rewarded by having the Temple (Beth Hamikdash) built in his territory.

Inaction

Sometimes people are judged for inaction, as was the case with Job, Jonah and Hezekiah.

According to the Midrash,[154] Pharaoh had three main advisors with whom he discussed his perceived Jewish problem: Bilaam; Yitro; and Job (Iyov). Bilaam advised Pharaoh to kill the Jews. Eventually Bilaam got his just desserts. He was killed by Pinhas. Yitro, Moses' future father in law, advised Pharaoh not to interfere with the Jews. He was forced to flee from Egypt to obscurity in Midian. His reward was that Moses married his daughter and his descendants served in the Temple. Job said nothing. His reward was that he would have to scream from pain and suffering (Job 2:7). Sometimes we are held responsible for inaction as well.

---

[151] Bereshit 37:32.
[152] Corresponding to the twenty-two years that Jacob was away from his parents, Rashi, Bereshit 37:34.
[153] Bereshit 44:33.
[154] Otzar Hamidrashim, Eisenstein, page 162.

God commanded Jonah to go to Nineveh and rebuke its inhabitants.[155] Jonah ran away in the opposite direction, but a person cannot run and hide from God. He was held accountable for his actions.

Hezekiah was king of the southern kingdom of Judah in 720 BCE. The Talmud (Sanhedrin 94a) says that he was the most ideally suited person to be Mashiach. His only fault was inaction. He failed to sing praises to God after witnessing amazing salvation.[156]

---

[155] Jonah 1:1.
[156] Kings 2, 19

Chapter 7. The Teshuvah Process

Just as we have to present our accounts to the tax authorities by April 15th each year, so too our spiritual accounts are examined by the Omnipotent Judge on Rosh Hashanah. This is the time of year that the Mishnah Rosh Hashanah 1:1 tells us is dedicated to the Divine judgment of mankind.

The ability to do Teshuvah is an extremely precious God-given gift that should not be scoffed at. It is totally irrational from a human perspective. How could a person be forgiven for a dastardly deed just by saying a few words and thinking a few thoughts? This is something that would never work in a human court of law.

Two Kinds of Teshuvah

What can teshuvah be compared to? Let us imagine that all our actions are recorded somewhere, as was mentioned earlier, and as is discussed in the Mishnah in Pirke Avot. We are, in essence, making a video recording of our lives, a movie in which the central character is us. Some of the unsavory episodes on the tape we regret making and would want deleted. Teshuvah allows us to: a) delete these unsavory episodes in our past. We can edit our tape erasing the bad episodes entirely or b) change the entire clip by re-recording it in a more favorable light.

These two kinds of teshuvah are known as: a) teshuvah from fear of God's punishment, which just erases the episode and leaves a blank segment in its wake, or b) teshuvah out of love of God; regret over our abuse of the gifts presented to us by loving, merciful God. This kind of teshuvah can change the entire episode on the tape for the better. It is a much higher level, only attainable by sincere penitents.

The Talmud in Avodah Zara 17-18 tells us about such cases. Among them it brings the tragic incident of Rabbi Chaninah Ben Tradion, who lived during one of the darkest periods in our history, that of the Roman persecution which followed the destruction of our second temple. Even though teaching Torah in public was illegal under Roman law, Rabbi Chaninah was determined to continue teaching until the end.

The story begins with the visit of Rabbi Chaninah to Rabbi Yossi Ben Kisma, who was ill. Rabbi Yossi, who was well-regarded in Roman circles, discusses Rabbi Chaninah's radical position of defying the Romans in public and rebukes him for putting his life in jeopardy in this manner. Rabbi Chaninah's response was that God would have mercy on him. Rabbi Yossi answered him, "I am telling you words of reason and you are telling me about mercy from heaven! I will be very surprised if they do not burn you and the Sefer Torah you use in fire." His dire warning fell on deaf ears and his unfortunate prediction soon came to pass.

When Rabbi Yossi died, the leaders of Rome went to his funeral to eulogize him. On the way back from the funeral, they saw Rabbi Chaninah Ben Tradion teaching a public Torah class with his Sefer Torah clutched to his chest. They wrapped the scroll around him and, placing wet wool near his torso to delay his death and cause more suffering, they set him on fire. One of the executioners asked Rabbi Chaninah that if he would hasten the Rabbi's death and prevent his suffering by removing the wet wool, would the Rabbi guarantee him a place in the World to Come. Rabbi Chaninah made this pledge, and the guard kept his word. Knowing that he would be executed for disobeying orders he also jumped into the fire and died.

A voice was heard, "Rabbi Chaninah Ben Tradion and the guard are welcome to the World to Come." Rabbi Judah the Prince, editor of the Mishnah, cried over the fact that the Roman executioner also acquired a place in the World to Come. "Some people acquire their place in the World to Come in one second, and some people only after many years of toil in God's service."

We see, from Rabbi Judah's comment, the power of teshuvah. In one second a person can earn their place in the future world, changing and breaking from their past.

We also see this idea referred to in the Talmud in Kiddushin 49b. The Talmud asks a question pertaining to the law of Jewish marriage. In those days it was common to make conditional marriages. When the condition was satisfied, then the marriage was considered valid. If the condition was not fulfilled, the marriage was considered not to have taken place. The Talmud asks about a case in which a young man known for his previous indiscretions makes the following condition: "You are sanctified to me on the condition that I am a Tzaddik." The Talmud answers that even if we are pretty sure that this particular gentleman was not a Tzaddik, nevertheless the marriage may be valid, since he may have done teshuvah in his mind. Even thoughts of repentance, of remorse and a commitment to change, are very important and can elevate a person immediately.

Making a U-turn

The following is another analogy dealing with teshuvah:

This author once was called upon to perform a wedding in a country club in upstate New York. The driving instructions were to turn off the New Jersey Turnpike one exit before the George Washington Bridge. Unfortunately this author missed the exit and found himself at the tolls leading to the bridge. Knowing the family involved to be very exact in their timing, the author started to panic, thinking of the consequences of his tardy arrival. If he would have to cross the bridge in heavy traffic and then make a U-turn, he would be at least an hour late to this very formal, expensive wedding. He explained the situation to the toll booth attendant, who very kindly offered to open the electric gate that was designed for emergencies, to allow him to make a U-turn before getting on the bridge. Fortunately the wedding was performed on time.

Teshuvah is a U-turn in our lives, and merciful God opens the gate to allow this U-turn.

A terribly vexing experience for a driver is to be speeding down a highway in the wrong direction, as sometimes happens. If a person is late for an appointment, they tend to speed. They miss a turn, and they end up speeding in the wrong direction, sometimes for miles, until the next turnoff.

Many of us in the world today are speeding down the highway of life in the wrong direction. We need to switch on our Divine GPS by attuning ourselves to the values of Torah.

Teshuvah is altering our course in life, as required to reach our final destination.

An Answer

Teshuvah can also mean an answer, - the answer to the most basic and deceptively simple question that God asks us. When Adam and Eve sinned by partaking of the fruit, they realized that they were naked, and made garments out of fig leaves. They heard God's presence and they hid among the trees of the garden and finally (Bereshit 3:9) they heard a one-word question, "Ayekka?" (Where are you?). The classical commentators, Rashi and Ibn Ezra, explain this question as God's way to start a conversation without scaring them, and giving them a way to admit their own faults without Him blaming them.

We find similar cases where God opened the conversation by asking a simple question:

a) In the case of Cain, after he killed his brother Abel, God opened the conversation by asking him where his brother was.[157]

b) In the case of Bilaam who was being approached by the messengers of Balak, King of Moab, to curse the Jews, God asks him very innocently, "Who are these people that are staying with you?"[158]

Included in this seemingly simple question of "Where are you?" which God asked Adam and Eve, is a deeper one. God is really asking them where they are holding, both spiritually and physically.

We have to envision God asking us the same question. Where are you? What are you doing with the precious life that God has given to you? To these and similar questions, we have to give a teshuvah, an answer.

Tzaddik, Rasha, and Benoni

Rambam, in Hilkhot Teshuvah, defines basic categories of people in order of merit:

1. A 'Tzaddik' (righteous person) is a person with more merits than demerits.

2. A 'Benoni' is a mediocre person whose merits and demerits are perfectly in balance. Imagine a person walking a tightrope over a large precipice. Think of the care he should take with each and every step of his way.

---

[157] Bereshit 4:9.
[158] Numbers 22.

3.   A 'Rasha' is an evil person who has more demerits than merits.

The system of God's justice, according to Rambam, is based not just on a person's quantity of good or bad deeds, which it may be possible to estimate, but also on the quality of the deeds, which only God can judge. In the Ethics of the Fathers, 2:1, Rabbi Judah the Prince says, "Be as careful with a small mitzvah as you would with a strict or large one because you don't know the reward for a mitzvah."

Just as we don't know the value of a mitzvah, so too we have no idea of the value of an aveirah (transgression); the beauty of this system is that it is impossible for anyone to gauge his or her own status in God's eyes. This uncertainty should make us try harder to improve ourselves.

If we are not able to quantify our own worth, then it is impossible for us to judge another person's worth, as is mentioned in Pirke Avot 1:6. Joshua Ben Perachia says, "Judge everyone favorably." We should aspire to judge oneself harshly and others favorably.

The Talmud[159] records a conversation Rabbi Yochanan Ben Zakkai had with his students when he was ill, just before his death. When he saw them, he started to cry. His students were amazed. "Light of all Israel, right-hand pillar, mighty hammer, why are you crying, surely you have nothing to worry about?" they asked him in wonder.

"My children," he responded, "If I was going for judgment before an earthly king whose life is temporary and his punishments were not eternal, maybe I would be able to pacify him with words and bribe him with money, I would still be terrified. How much more so that I am going before the King of Kings, the Holy One blessed is He, who lives eternally. If He gets angry, His anger is forever.

---

[159] Berachot 28b.

If He jails me, His jail is forever. If He kills me, my death will be forever. I cannot pacify Him with words or bribe Him with money. Furthermore, there are two paths before me, one leads to Gan Eden and one to Gehinam, and I don't know which way they are leading me. Shouldn't I cry?"

"Rabbi, please bless us!" they cried.

The great sage responded "May your fear of God be like your fear of man." was his blessing.

"Is that all?"[160] They exclaimed.

"I wish that it would be so." was his rejoinder. "Know that when a person transgresses, he says 'Nobody sees me.'"[161]

If Rabbi Yochanan Ben Zakkai, on his tremendously high level, was uncertain about his own fate, we certainly have no idea where we stand in God's infinite justice system.

Rambam advocates that all of us view ourselves continually as *Benonim*, neither evil nor good, but in the middle. One good deed will push the scales onto the side of righteousness and one bad deed would push us into the abyss. If we could only continually internalize this very simple thought, that we are teetering on the edge, that a small good deed can tip the scales to the side of merit and vice-versa, it is certain that this would have a tremendous positive impact on our lives.

---

[160] They were surprised that he equated the fear of God with the fear of man, and felt that it was not enough of a blessing.

[161] Most people are concerned that others shouldn't witness their evil deeds, but are not concerned that God witnesses everything.

Admission, The First Stage of Repentance

The first stage of the teshuvah process is viduy or admission of past mistakes. Just as a doctor cannot treat a patient who refuses to admit to being sick, so too the repentance process cannot even begin without this seemingly small step of admitting that one is at fault. On the surface this may seem to be a small step, but the truth is that it takes a great person to admit his or her shortcomings, even to him or herself.

Mental Image, - Pride and Humility

We all have an image of ourselves in our minds. We tend to view ourselves according to that image. The Talmud[162] states that a person is related to him/herself. Just as a relative's testimony is not admissible as evidence in a Jewish court, so too a person's own testimony for or against himself is inadmissible as evidence.

If a person is proud, his or her mental picture of him or herself is bigger than what he or she actually is. Adjusting this picture to make it smaller is a very painful process. Ego is a very big problem, as it hides our true selves and presents an exaggerated image of who we are.

False humility is the other extreme. It presents a smaller picture of who we truly are, causing a loss of equilibrium to the person and sometimes even depression. In severe cases, it is very difficult to alter the awful self-image that depressed people have of themselves in their own minds.

Look at the different responses of the first two kings of all the twelve tribes, Saul and David, to censure.[163] When rebuked by the prophet Samuel (Samuel 1, 15:19), King Saul denied responsibility for

---

[162] Yebamot 25b.

[163] Saul's son, Ish Boshet, did reign for a period of two years but not over the tribe of Judah.

any wrongdoing, rationalizing and blaming others for his failings. King David, however, when confronted by the prophet Nathan regarding his affair with Batsheva,[164] immediately admitted his sin. This was the greatness of the Davidic line of Kings, the greatness of character to be able to admit to faults and failures. This is why the dynasty of David survived even after the Batsheva episode, since he recognized and admitted his failings and tried to change.

The Talmud[165] states that only Kings of the Davidic line may be judged by the Sanhedrin (the high court), because only they were great enough to admit their faults. This law was made after the following incident:

> A slave of King Yannai (one of the Maccabean Kings) killed someone. Rabbi Shimon Ben Shetach said to the Rabbis of the Sanhedrin, "Judge him." They sent a message to Yannai "Your servant has killed someone. Send him to us for judgment." He sent the servant. They sent him another message that he, the King also had to come to trial, since he was responsible for the actions of his servant. The King came and sat in front of the court. Shimon Ben Shetach told him to stand on his feet, saying, "You are standing before God." Yannai refused to rise, and the other members of the Sanhedrin would not enforce this. The Talmud concludes that all the other members of the Sanhedrin were eventually wiped out.

King David's readiness to admit his faults was a trait inherited from his forefather Judah, after whom the tribe was named. Judah's Hebrew name consists of the same letters as those of God's four letter name, with an additional 'Dalet'. This 'Dalet' stands for 'Dalut,' humility.

---

[164] Samuel 2. 12:13.
[165] Sanhedrin 19a.

The Bible,[166] after discussing Joseph's arrival in Egypt, compares his saintly behavior in captivity with that of his brother Judah, who was ultimately responsible for his plight. Joseph resisted the blandishments of his master Potiphar's wife, time after time, earning the title Joseph the Tzaddik. Judah succumbed to the temptation of a temporary, gratuitous relationship.

Judah took a wife for his oldest son Er, called Tamar. Er died and Judah followed the then-accepted custom[167] of levirate marriage. He gave Tamar to wed his second son, Onan. His son Onan also died.[168] Judah balked at then giving Tamar to his youngest son, Shelah, afraid that somehow Tamar was involved in the death of the first two sons. He sent Tamar home to her parents with the excuse that his younger son Shelah was too young to marry. She waited for him to keep his implied promise of levirate marriage, albeit in vain.

Tamar then took matters into her own hands. She dressed as a prostitute and seduced her father-in-law, Judah, without his knowing who she was. She conceived from this single encounter, and was brought before the judge for trial on the charge of adultery. Technically she was considered married to Shelah, as levirate marriage was automatic and did not require a formal ceremony.

The judge was none other than her father-in-law, Judah. His verdict for her crime was death by burning. Before removing her from the courtroom to carry out the sentence, he asked her if she had anything to say in her defense. She showed him the things he had given her as collateral, in lieu of payment, on the night of their relations and very simply said, "I am pregnant by the man that these things belong to."

---

[166] Bereshit, Chapter 38.

[167] It appears that this was an accepted custom even before the Torah was given.

[168] As a result of spilling his 'seed' – Onanism, see the biblical commentaries for a fuller account of what transpired.

Judah could have had her burned and no one would have been the wiser. Instead, he admitted his fault in public "Tzadka mimeni" - she is more righteous than me. He had the greatness of character to acknowledge his blunder and make amends with Tamar, thus sparing her life and those of the twins in her womb from which came the Davidic line of Kings, and ultimately will come the Messiah.

It is hard to admit ones failings. We are all biased in our own favor and we do not hesitate to rationalize when necessary.

An Honest Accounting

An honest accounting is required, and this can be very painful and psychologically disturbing, a kind of spiritual exploratory surgery. We have to examine various important ingredients of our lives. A by no means exhaustive list should definitely include the following:

1. Our deeds.
2. Our motives.
3. Our relations with others (bein adam le chavero).
4. Our influence on others: good or bad?
5. The influence of others on us: good or bad?
6. The direction of our lives - We have to ask ourselves whether we are moving closer to the Divine or further away. And finally, the million dollar question:
7. What is our potential (see Chapter 10), and are we living up to it?

The Second stage of the Repentance Process - Regret

The next stage in the teshuvah process, and probably the most painful, which it should be, is the process of regret: remorse for (a) what was, and (b) what could have been.

While we know the impact of what was, and we can imagine the consequences, we cannot even begin to imagine what could have been. See the discussion in Chapter 10 regarding potential.

Regret or what is called in common parlance a 'guilt trip' should be painful. The more painful it is, the greater the likelihood that the person will change.

Just as a person who has a disease of the nervous system and feels no pain is at tremendous risk of inflicting grievous injury on himself, so too a person whose spiritual nervous system does not function as it should and feels no spiritual pain or guilt is at risk of causing the soul grievous injury. We have to work on magnifying the regret to a point where the pain will be too great for us to even consider repeating the act. This leads to the third stage of the process.

The Third Aspect of Repentance, Commitment to Change

The third aspect of true teshuvah is that of making a firm unshakable resolution to never repeat past mistakes. A person who will never repeat past mistakes is a genuine baal teshuvah. A genuine baal teshuvah has undergone such a vast change that he or she seems like a new person. He or she can hardly be recognized by neighbors and friends. This is really the significance of the change of name ceremony for a very ill person. It symbolizes that the person has changed their outlook on life for the better and is thus not worthy of being treated by heaven in this manner. A baal teshuvah should be like a convert who receives a new name at the time of conversion, which shows the beginning of a new phase of his or her life.

Rambam defines a baal teshuvah as someone who still yearns for the things he/she sinned with previously. He/she is still is in the same physical condition as before, with the same amount of desire for the deed, but when faced with a similar trial controls him/herself because of repentance.

One of the most commonly misunderstood accounts in the Torah is the story of Joseph. At first glance it appears to be a classic tale of petty jealousy, vindictiveness and vengeance However, this is not the true picture. The classic penitents (baalei teshuvah) mentioned explicitly in the Five Books of Moses (Chumash) were the brothers of Joseph. Joseph, in turn, is known as the righteous one (Tzaddik) because he had no thought of taking revenge on them. He could have easily tortured and annihilated them at his convenience. Instead, he supported them and their large families with food and lodging to the end of his days.

We know that ten of Joseph's brothers hated him. There were four causes for this hatred mentioned explicitly in the text:

a) His mother had been favored over theirs.
b) He had spoken gossip about them.[169]
c) He was his father's favorite. This caused tremendous jealousy and ill-feeling.[170]
d) He had egotistic dreams.[171]

In the first part of the story, the brothers did not repent and desired to rid themselves of the troublemaker. We do, however, see that despite their burning anger toward Joseph, his brothers continually lessened the severity of their planned actions as follows:

1. First they planned to kill Joseph outright and throw his dead body in a pit.[172] The Midrash states that this was the suggestion of his brother Simon, and that is why Joseph held Simon in jail when he sent the other brothers home the first time.

---

[169] Bereshit 37:2.
[170] Bereshit 37:4.
[171] Bereshit 37:10.
[172] Bereshit 37:20

2. Then Reuben, the oldest, persuaded them not to kill him, but to throw him in the pit alive. His intention was to save him later. Ramban points out that the Torah later[173] records Reuben as accusing his brothers of not listening to him when he tried to stop them from harming Joseph. Obviously he had tried unsuccessfully to dissuade them from hurting their brother. Throwing him into the pit was a compromise between Reuben and them.

3. Then, Judah suggested that instead of killing their brother even indirectly, he be sold to the Yishmaelite merchants who were passing by.

Each time, they reconsidered their actions and controlled them. This is an important technique that we all have to learn. We may get a burning impulse to do something, but how do we control and reduce this impetus? The brothers obviously had a great desire to harm Joseph, but gradually controlled this inclination.

This is a big lesson for us. Even if a person is going to sin, they should at least try their best to diminish the enormity of the sin.

Incidentally, the Torah does not explicitly say that the brothers sold him. It only says that they wanted to sell him. The majority of commentators do say that the brothers did the selling. However, Rashbam[174] explains that the brothers could not stand to hear the cries of Joseph and moved out of earshot. While they were away the Yishmaelites took him out of the pit and sold him to the Midianites. This explains Reuben's astonishment and despair when he came back to find Joseph gone from the pit. When the Torah later on quotes Joseph as saying that the brothers had sold him, what he meant was that they, through their actions, had caused him to be sold.

---

[173] Bereshit 42:22.

[174] Rabbi Shlomo Ben Meir, 12th century France. Bible and Talmud commentator and a grandson of Rashi.

Later on, the brothers were sent down to Egypt to buy food during a famine. Joseph had matured and become the successful viceroy of Egypt. They had no idea that he was the one standing before them. Joseph accused them of being spies and locked them in jail for three days. He finally let them out, except for Simon, with a stern warning not to come back unless they brought Benjamin, their youngest brother, back with them.

We find the first stage of teshuvah in their admission (Bereshit 42:21) "But we are guilty for our brother. We saw the pain of his soul and we didn't listen to his pleas. That is why this trouble has come upon us."

Reuben then rebuked them, "Didn't I tell you not to sin to the boy? But you did not listen and now his blood is being avenged." Not one of them objected to his rebuke. This was an expression of regret, which they all took to heart.

On the way back, they found that the money they had given to the Egyptians for the food that they had bought was returned with their purchases, and they trembled with fear. "What has God done to us?" they asked each other. This was pure, unadulterated, psychological suffering. This caused them terrible trepidation, which was a partial atonement for them.

On their second trip back to Egypt for more food, they brought Benjamin, as Joseph had instructed. We see that Joseph had only good intentions toward them. His mercy was aroused by their woeful presence. In Genesis 43:30 he cried for their pain. He treated Benjamin with great favoritism, reminding them of their father's great love and favoritism toward him, giving them an excuse to hate Benjamin as they had once hated him. Joseph was setting them up with a trial to see whether they would abandon Benjamin as they had abandoned him earlier.

Joseph had his special cup planted in Benjamin's sack and then sent his men after them to retrieve his cup. The brothers were aghast at his accusation that one of them had stolen his special cup. They were so sure that none of them would ever do such a thing that they vowed death to the person in whose sack the cup was found. When it was found in Benjamin's sack, they had the perfect opportunity to abandon him, as they had abandoned Joseph years earlier. However, they refused to let Benjamin be taken into slavery, and they all accompanied him back to Joseph to defend him and plead for him. This is the fourth stage of Teshuvah, - passing a test. They passed this test with flying colors. Only then, when Joseph was assured of their total repentance and change of attitude, did he reveal himself to them.

We see that Joseph was setting the stage for their perfect Teshuvah. He was their 'Teshuvah facilitator'.

The Fourth Aspect of Repentance, Trials

Although trials are necessary for complete repentance and for spiritual growth, we pray to God every day in the morning blessings to lead us neither in the path of trial nor in the path of disgrace.' We don't want trials because they could end in disgrace of failure. Not everyone is as well developed in their fear of heaven to be able to withstand temptation.

The Talmud[175] contemplated this issue when discussing the conversation which took place between God and King David. David asked God why the Amidah (the silent standing prayer) starts off with the line 'Blessed are you Lord, God of our fathers, God of Abraham, God of Isaac and God of Jacob'. King David asked God why his name is not mentioned in the opening paragraph of the Amidah. God's answer was that the forefathers were tried and trusted. They had passed their trials whereas he hadn't. King David

---

[175] Sanhedrin 107a.

asked for a trial,[176] which he then failed. His trial was Batsheva. We should never ask to be tested by God because the odds of our passing the test are not favorable.

The Levels of Sin

Rambam lists the steps in the forgiveness process. With respect to these steps, he divides the mitzvot into four categories.

1. Positive commandments for which there is no 'karet'. An example would be a person who purposely did not recite the Grace after Meals (Birkat Hamazon) after having a satisfying meal, which is a biblical positive commandment. As is stated, "You will eat, be satisfied, and bless..."[177] If the person who skipped Grace after Meals sincerely says to God: "I am sorry for not thanking you properly for the food. From now on I will be careful to say grace every time I eat." Then, God's complete forgiveness is immediately granted.

2. Negative commandments for which there is no 'karet'. Two steps are required for complete forgiveness: a. teshuvah b. the passing of Yom Kippur. An example would be a person who spoke evil or gossip about someone else. To obtain forgiveness from God, he or she would have to make the following statement: "I am sorry for breaking the commandment of not tale bearing. I will never do it again." Forgiveness is only received after the next Yom Kippur passes.[178]

---

[176] Psalms 26:2.

[177] Deuteronomy 8:10. There is no punishment for violation of this command mentioned in the Torah.

[178] Another example of this would be where a person cooked milk and meat together in the same pot. Even though he did not taste it, he transgressed the biblical injunction of not cooking a kid goat in its mother's milk. To obtain forgiveness from God, he or she would have to make the following statement: "I am sorry for breaking the commandment of not cooking meat with milk. I will never do it again."

3. Positive and negative commandments for which there is a Karet penalty. Three steps are required in order to obtain cleansing: a. Teshuvah. b. the passing of Yom Kippur. c. Yissurim, or troubles. The person must go through an additional process of pain and suffering, depending on the seriousness of the sin. For example, a person who ate a slice of bread on Passover (Pesach), with no extenuating circumstances, transgressed a negative command for which there is Karet.

4. Chillul Hashem - The desecration of God's name . In the eyes of the masses, whether we like it or not, a Jew, especially a religious one, is God's ambassador in the world. When such a person sins in public, it causes a Chillul Hashem. The forgiveness process for Chillul Hashem includes the following four steps: a. Teshuvah. b. The passing of Yom Kippur. c. Pain and suffering. Forgiveness is only complete with d. Death.

Chapter 8. Success

What is the definition of success? We all have our own ideas. In today's Western-dominated culture, the answer is money, pleasure, power and prestige. It is ingrained into us from an early age that these are the values to strive for.

A contemporary Rabbi once asked his students the following question: "Who is wealthier, a person with one dollar or a person with two dollars?" The students were baffled that the Rabbi would ask them a question with such an obvious answer. The Rabbi guessed what was perplexing them and answered the question himself. "The person with one dollar thinks in terms of a single dollar and therefore wants another dollar, to double what he already has. The individual with two dollars also wants to double what he has and therefore wants another two dollars. The latter, in his own mind, has greater needs than the former person, and is therefore poorer."

The Midrash in Kohelet Rabbah 1 puts the pursuit of material desires in very bleak terms. 'A person does not die with even half of their desires in their hands.' Whatever we have, we want to double. A person who has a hundred dollars thinks in terms of hundreds. A person who has thousands, starts thinking in terms of tens of thousands. A person who has tens of thousands starts to think in terms of hundreds of thousands, and a person who has millions starts thinking about his next million. He is therefore poorest, as in his own reckoning he lacks a million.

Our perspectives change according to our circumstances. This concept is described by Maimonides at the end of Hilkhot Teshuvah (Chapter 10) and in his famous Eight Chapters on the Eleventh Chapter of Sanhedrin. Maimonides discusses how to motivate different types of people to serve God. We are able to motivate young children with small gifts, like candies. When the child grows and matures, the gifts have to grow and have to measure up to his expectations. An adult will not be satisfied with the same category of gifts that he received when he was younger he expects more. We see that as we mature our material standards and aspirations change.

Material wealth, power, and prestige do not quench the thirst for more. Instead, they whet a person's appetite by raising expectations.

The Bible discusses three tremendously wealthy individuals who were not at peace with themselves and strove for more, causing their own destruction: Adam, Haman and Bilaam.

The Talmud in Chullin 139b asks where Haman's name is alluded to in the Torah. The Talmud answers that Haman is alluded to in a verse in Genesis 3:11 when God asks Adam: "Have you eaten of the tree from which I commanded you not to eat?" the word 'Hamin' in the verse has the same Hebrew letters as the word Haman. The Talmud seems to be pointing out that there is a link between Haman and Adam. What could this link be?

Both Haman and Adam were blessed with material success. Adam, especially, was the guardian and owner of the whole known world and its natural resources, Haman was second in command to the King of one of the largest empires the world has ever known. This great wealth was not enough for either of them. They were not satisfied.

The one thing that God withheld from Adam was the fruit of the tree of knowledge (Genesis 2:17). Everything else was given to him, and yet, when the time came, he could not resist the temptation to partake of the forbidden fruit. The wealthiest man ever was not satisfied, even though only one thing was beyond his grasp. He wanted it, and risked everything he had for it.

Haman[179] after recounting his great wealth and importance to his relatives and friends says, "Yet all this is worth nothing to me so long as I see Mordechai the Jew sitting at the King's gate." Everything he had was worthless. He wanted Mordechai the Jew dead, even though a decree had already been promulgated to exterminate all the Jews including Mordechai (3: 13). He was not willing to wait at all. He wanted it and he wanted it now!

Both Adam and Haman came to tragic ends. Adam was removed from the Garden of Eden, losing his luxurious elevated lifestyle, and was cursed to earn his bread by the sweat of his brow. Haman was eventually killed by the King for plotting the destruction of Mordechai, the savior of the King.

Bilaam was a gentile prophet.[180] He was hired by Balak the King of Moab to curse the Jewish People. God warned him several times not to go with the agents of Balak. Even though he was already very wealthy and famous, the lure of more money and prestige was irresistible. Bilaam went with the agents of Balak and came to his ultimate destruction at the hands of Pinhas.

This is a moral for our generation, especially the 'me generation' of instant gratification.

Material success does not always bring happiness.

To define success in physical terms is extremely difficult. Even though in theory the world is limited, as far as individuals are concerned, who can have it all? Even if one has it all, for how long can he/she have it? Nobody is here forever. How much of the pie does a person have to have in order to be called successful? How big does his or her house, or houses, have to be? What kind of a

---

[179] Book of Esther (5:11-13)
[180] See Numbers 22

car does he or she have to drive? Success is subjective, if we do not bring God into the picture.

A person may be very successful by third-world standards, as we all are. We take our luxuries for granted, ignoring and not appreciating them. If someone were to visit us from some third-world country, their eyes would pop out of their heads. They would be amazed at the size of our houses, our carpets, our beds and furniture, sinks, bathrooms and running water, even hot water, and heating systems. If we were to be measured by their standards, we would all be considered to be princes and princesses. However, we measure success by our own standards and compare our achievements with those of our more 'successful' neighbors.

Two Definitions of Success

1. King Solomon, reputedly the wisest of all men, was also probably the expert in physical pleasure. He had a thousand wives, many palaces, armies of servants, and gold and silver that flowed like water. In his book, Kohelet, translated as Ecclesiastes, he examined physical existence. With all his wealth, he came to the conclusion in Kohelet 1:1 that 'Vanity of vanities, all is vanity.' At the end of this book, in Kohelet 12:13, he reaches the realization that 'The end of the matter is, fear God and keep his commandments, because this is what man is about.' This is spiritual success.

2. In Pirke Avot 4:1 there is a beautiful saying, "Who is a wealthy person? A person who is happy with his portion." In other words, material wealth is totally subjective. If a person is content, then in his own eyes he is successful. This is emotional, spiritual and physical success.

There is a mitzvah in the Torah to say grace after meals.[181] 'You will eat and be satisfied and bless the Lord your God...' The mitzvah from the Torah is that only a person who was satisfied from the meal has to say the blessing. However, the Rabbis later ordained that even one who ate the equivalent of an olive-size of bread should say grace after meals. I think that the Torah is teaching us a very important idea: that only a person who is satisfied from his eating should praise God. A person who ate only a small amount and was satisfied has to say the grace after meals, whereas a person who ate a lot and is still not satisfied should not praise God.

The Almighty does not want praise from someone who is not satisfied, however much he or she ate and enjoyed. A person who is never satisfied can never say a blessing.

Rambam writes that for health reasons a person should never eat enough to fill his stomach, but should leave a quarter of it empty because many illnesses are caused from overeating. If so, one might ask, according to Rambam, would a person never be obligated from Torah law to say grace after meals? What Rambam is stating is that there are two separate things:

a) The satisfaction of the stomach. For health reasons a person should not fill his or her stomach.

b) The satisfaction of the mind on which the obligation of grace after meals is dependent. This should be achieved prior to the stomach being satisfied.

The Rabbis in the Talmud contrasted the popular view of life with their own world view. When a baby is born, people laugh, and when a person dies people cry. It should be the other way around. When a child is born we should cry. After all, we don't know what this precious soul will achieve in its lifetime. When a person dies we should rejoice. If that soul had fulfilled its

---

[181] Deuteronomy 8:10

purpose in life there is no greater achievement possible, and nothing more worthy of enjoyment.

Diversions from Success

The Hafetz Haim related a parable as to what this world is all about. A King's daughter was very sick and no cure could be found for her illness. The King announced that the person who could heal his daughter would be rewarded with a day in his treasury, where he could help himself to whatever he wanted. A person was finally able to cure the princess, and the day of his reward came. He arrived early in the morning with empty sacks, ready to carry away the treasures he was so sure of obtaining.

The King being no fool was not in a rush to lose all his precious treasures, and had arranged a diversion. After putting jewelry into the sacks for about half an hour, the man started hearing the strains of an orchestra playing. He had a weakness for music, especially this kind of music. He was drawn to it and came out of the treasury to find the source of the music. He drew closer and found that a wonderful party was taking place, with all kinds of culinary delights and other attractions. He decided to check out this party. After all, he had the whole day left to gather precious items from the treasury.

After eating and drinking and dancing to the wonderful music, he nearly forgot his purpose in coming to the King's palace that day. He was abruptly reminded by the sound of the big clock chiming six o' clock. He rushed back to the treasury but after an hour was forced out by the King's guards. "Sorry sir, your time is up." They told him. He left the treasury with his small sack half full, and wished he had made more time for the essential task at hand. Outside, a large crowd of partygoers had gathered to humiliate him. "Didn't you realize that this diversion was set up by the King?" They asked him. He grinned back sheepishly, wishing that he could hide in some corner. He was ashamed of having been tricked so easily.

The Hafetz Haim says that this parable represents what is going on in this world. God put us here for a purpose, to gather the precious treasures of as many good deeds as we can. Unfortunately, we get sidetracked by what other people consider success and we forget about our mission and enjoy ourselves in the party of life.

The Hafetz Haim gives another insightful parable as to the consequences of our mistake regarding what success is all about. A person left his home country to go abroad on business. He took with him a sheaf of paper currency to carry to that country. When he got to his destination, he was shocked to find that his money was not accepted anywhere. It was the wrong currency. Throughout our lives we work hard for physical things. We may eventually be surprised to find that the physical currency we have acquired is worthless in the next world.

The Prerequisites for Success

There is no question that an important ingredient for achieving success is to have the basic commodities for a person to live on. Health, strength, brains, food, clothing, and shelter all are undeniably necessary for human existence.

The blessing that the brothers Jacob and Esau fought over (Genesis 27:28) turned out to be physical in nature and included the following elements:

a) Sustenance.
b) Respect from others
c) Peace in the family under the blessed party's leadership.
d) Peace of mind.

The priestly blessing recited every day in the synagogue includes the following ingredients of Divine blessing:

    a) Protection, safety.
    b) God's grace.
    c) God's favor.
    d) Peace.

When Moses blessed his disciple Joshua (Deuteronomy 31), his main emphasis was on strength of character.

There is a beautiful story in Kings I. 3:9. When God told the young King Solomon that he could ask for whatever he desired and He would grant it to him, the young king asked for wisdom to understand good and evil in order to judge his people. God was extremely pleased with his choice and blessed him with understanding, wealth, honor, and long life.

The Midrash brings a parable to elucidate God's reward to Solomon. If a person is offered a single wish from a mortal king (to ask for whatever he desires), the Midrash says he should ask for the king's only daughter's hand in marriage. Whoever marries the king's daughter is assured of being the next king, so too a person who asks for wisdom is assured of obtaining everything else.

In fact, the first personal prayer that we utter three times daily in the 'Amidah' is the fourth blessing, which is the prayer for wisdom and understanding. This has always been a Jewish emphasis and priority throughout the ages. "Brains over brawn" has always been an integral part of Jewish existence over the millennia.

Millennia ago, the Jews were the first people to insist on an education for every single child up to Bar Mitzvah age. Over 20% of Nobel Prize winners have been Jewish, even though Jews make up less than 0.01% of the world's population.

Knowledge is a basic ingredient, even for material success. A popular saying has always been that "A fool and his money are easily parted."

The Mishnah, in Pirke Avot 2:5, states that an ignorant person cannot be pious. True piety, the kind that is not based on mere superstition, presupposes an understanding of the nature of the world and knowledge of what God requires from us. This then is our first petition to God, which has priority over all other choices, and is the main key to success.

The next provision for success is repentance (teshuvah), which we have previously discussed. Teshuvah is a cleansing of one's conscience, which leads to peace of mind and draws us closer to our Creator. We human beings are constantly in inner turmoil. Our passions and desires can wreak havoc on us. Peace of mind is one of the prerequisites for success.

Personality Development for Success

The following Torah principles are involved in personality development for success.

1. Be Joyful

King David in Psalms 100:2 advises us to 'Serve God with joy.' The Talmud in Pesahim 117a states that the Divine spirit does not rest on a person who is depressed or worried, or on a person who is boisterous, but only on someone who is possessed of the quiet joyfulness that flows from God's commandments. The biblical story of King Saul (Samuel 1. 16:23) illustrates the idea of the importance of being joyful. King Saul had fits of depression and would employ musicians, among whom was the future King David, to play music for him to cheer him up.

2. A Positive Attitude - Have Faith in God

A person should always maintain a positive attitude. This is achieved by finding the good even in bad events and happenings. The Mishnah in Berachot 60b tells us to bless God for bad news, just as we bless on the good news. Even bad things have positive elements to them. Many times only God in his wisdom knows that this is the case. Those directly involved may not be able to see any good at all.

God tests those who can grow through the trial. It is hard to be submissive, doubly hard when we are wracked by troubles that we don't really believe we deserve. A person's troubles may cause disintegration of his resources at the very moment when he most needs them.

There are two main perspectives related to this issue mentioned in the Talmud, that of Rabbi 'Nachum Ish Gam Zu' and that of his student of twenty-two years, Rabbi Akiva.[182] Legend has it that when Akiva the shepherd decided, with the encouragement of his wife Rachel, to go and learn Torah, he had difficulty finding a Rabbi because the first question he would be asked was, "Do you know how to read?" When he would answer in the negative, he was sent away from the academy. When he was asked this question by Rabbi 'Nachum Ish Gam Zu' and answered in the negative, the reply he received from the famed Rabbi shocked everyone around, "Gam Zu Le-Tovah!" (Even this will be for the best).

Rabbi 'Nachum Ish Gam Zu' earned his name from this, his favorite saying. Many times, bad things happen that we are unable to explain. They appear to us to have no good element in them at all. Rabbi Nachum would say that even such a bad event is good. God is loving, kind and merciful, then even bad things have a good reason and purpose.

---

[182] Chagigah 12a.

Rabbi Nachum saw the advantages of shepherd Akiva's ignorance. His lack of knowledge of the most basic rubrics of Judaism would allow him to apply his maturity and wisdom of years to even simple things, like the alphabet which most people, having been brought up with it from youth, take for granted. In fact, we find that a book was written by Rabbi Akiva on the significance and symbolism of the Hebrew letters, called Otiot d'Rabbi Akiva (Letters of Rabbi Akiva).

The second advantage was that Akiva's mature mind would analyze every single letter and word in the Torah, something that children, when they learn Torah, do not do. As a result when they grow up they have already taken the format of the Torah for granted. Rabbi Akiva, together with his master of twenty two years, were famous for knowing the reasons for every extra and missing letter (Shevuot 26a) and for every extra word, notably the word 'et.' (See Talmud Chagigah 12a).

The third advantage of Akiva's age and ignorance was that his mature and questioning mind would focus on small elements of detail that a child and someone who was used to the text from youth would miss. The Talmud Menachot 29b relates that Rabbi Akiva learned thousands of laws from the significance of the little crowns (taggim) found on certain letters of the sefer Torah.

Indeed, Rabbi Nachum was truly correct when he told the shepherd Akiva, "Even this will be for the best." It is thanks to his positive attitude of treating his elderly student with respect and hope that one of the biggest stars in the Jewish firmament was created. It is from Rabbi Akiva and his five main students that the vast body of Jewish oral law is derived.

The Talmud (Berachot 60b) also relates a beautiful story of Rabbi Akiva, who followed closely in attitude to that of his master. Rabbi Akiva's maxim was slightly different from that of his master, "Kol de avid Rachmana letab avid" (Whatever God does is for the best).

One day Rabbi Akiva was traveling to a distant place. It was getting dark when he arrived at a small town to break his journey and stay the night. In those days, the towns had walls around them to protect them from all sorts of dangers. When he arrived at the town, he found that the gates had already been closed. Even the prestige of his name was not enough to open the gates to allow his entry. People were afraid of a ruse by the Romans, who were currently wreaking havoc on surrounding towns in the vicinity. Rabbi Akiva was therefore forced to spend the night in the fields. He reacted to this with equanimity. "Whatever God does is for the best," he muttered to himself. He found a secluded spot away from the town in a verdant field to spend the night. His mode of transport was a donkey, which he tethered to a bush nearby. In the middle of the night, a predator came and devoured it. Rabbi Akiva's reaction was "Whatever God does is for the best." He was now left without transport and would have to travel the long distance on foot.

His rooster, which he relied upon to arouse him at the first sign of dawn, was likewise devoured, and he was left without an alarm clock. His reaction was the same. Finally a strong gust of wind blew and put out his lantern. "Whatever happens is for the best."

The next morning he went to the town and was aghast to find that it was a smoking pile of burning rubble. The Romans had totally destroyed it that night. Now he understood the events of the past night and thanked God for saving him.

The moral of all this is that we can only see segments of the total picture, just as a person who watches the final part of a movie may wonder why a particular event took place out of context. He or she will only understand the plot by watching the whole movie. So too it is hard for us to judge by just viewing one segment of the plot and outcome of the whole movie of our lives. We have to believe that whatever happens to us, outside of our own free will, is part of God's total plan for us and for the whole of creation. The Midrash[183] therefore emphasizes that a person should frequently say that whatever is caused by Heaven is for the good.

Troubles must lead to introspection. When we fall victim to misfortune, we need to examine our actions closely. The likelihood is that we will not come up empty-handed. If we do, we must assume that our commitment to Torah learning was not what it should have been.[184]

Not everyone's reaction to troubles and tribulations can be as pure as that of Rabbi Nachum 'Ish Gam Zu' and Rabbi Akiva. There are two other different reactions to trials and tribulation mentioned in the Torah:

The reaction of Moses (Moshe Rabenu) to the increased persecution of the Jewish people after God had sent him to save them (at the end of Parashat Shemot, Exodus 5:22,23), when he questions his mission: "And Moses returned to God and said, 'Lord, for what reason have you allotted misfortune to this people? Why did You send me? For, since I came to Pharaoh to speak in your name, he has treated the people badly, and You haven't delivered the people.' "

This way of questioning God's providence is mirrored on a personal level by the events of the book of Job. Job suffers terribly. He lost his wealth, children, and finally his health, and was wracked by terrible pain. He questions God. Is it all right to question? Yes. That is the short answer, which the long and complex saga of Job teaches us. Job struggled and fought and challenged and asked over and over again, "Why?" In the end, God said that he spoke

---

[183] Otzar Hamidrashim Eisenstein, Page 270.
[184] Berachot 5a.

well, better than his friends who thought that they had all the answers.[185]

The prophet Habakkuk demanded an explanation for the chaos that he observed, and for which he could find no excuses.[186] It is all right to question, all right to challenge when question and challenge are rooted in emunah (faith in God and his goodness). However, it is never permitted to rebel.

The second way of dealing with troubles was that of Aaron Hacohen (The Priest), the brother of Moses. Aaron had lost his two sons, Nadab and Abihu, during the ceremony to dedicate the sanctuary (Leviticus 10). His response was a purposeful silence. He never questioned God's actions. This was also the way of the forefathers, who never complained to God about their trials. All they had from God were empty promises. They never saw any fulfillment. Rather, their faith was tested even more. For example, Abraham was promised the land of Canaan. As soon as he got there, there was a tremendous famine and he had to leave. When he went to Egypt, his wife was kidnapped. When his wife died, he had to pay an exorbitant amount of money for a place to bury her. Abraham never asked any questions. Even when he was told to raise up his beloved son Isaac, he did not ask questions. That was his greatness.

Acute suffering can sometimes generate corrosive morbidity, or equally injurious, misplaced and ultimately destructive belligerence. Both are essentially healthy reactions taken to unacceptable extremes. Not everyone can be a Nachum Ish Gam Zu, who reveled in the sheer horror of his destitution.[187]

We might wish, when we are plagued with questions, that our faith was stronger, purer, less subject to questioning God, which

---

[185] Job 42:7.

[186] Habakkuk 1:2-3.

[187] Taanit 21a.

gives us no peace. The Aaron mode might suit us more than that which Job legitimized. But Job, in the end, met God and found vindication.

3. Love Your Friend as Yourself

What do we do about life's challenges? In our daily morning prayers, we ask God not to put us to the test. If we can remain cheerful, positive, and trusting in God until the very end, we will certainly have passed the test of troubles and tribulations, and this is an important key to success. The Talmud[188] relates the following interesting story of a pagan who came to Shammai and asked to convert to Judaism, but only on the condition that he was taught the whole Torah within the period of time that he could remain standing on one foot. Shammai thought that the pagan was belittling Judaism and his response was abruptly negative. Fortunately the pagan then went to Hillel. Hillel's response was the passive expression of Leviticus 16:18 'Love your friend[189] as yourself': "Don't do to others what you don't want others to do to you. This is the whole Torah. The rest is all commentary, go and learn." The man eventually converted to Judaism.

Rabbi Akiva sums it up, "'Love your friend as yourself,' is an important rule in the Torah."[190] This is a very important part of success in life, not to be involved in petty quarrels and disputes, which eat a person up at night and do not allow them to sleep. One of the secrets of success is developing love for others, and avoiding bearing grudges, vengeance, resentment or hostility.

There are other commandments in the Torah that mirror these values. 'Do not take vengeance on your brother,' is an example. There are two types of vengeance mentioned,[191] which have been

---

[188] Shabbat 31a.
[189] Usually mistranslated as 'neighbor.'
[190] Sifra Kedoshim, Parashah 2.
[191] Leviticus 19:18.

explained by the Talmud[192] as: a physical tit-for-tat; "You wouldn't lend me your ax, so I won't lend you my shovel." Or as a verbal vengeance or reservation; "Here is my shovel, even though you didn't lend me your ax. I am not like you." The person who avoids these thoughts will live a healthy and happy life.

4. Think Positively About Others

The rabbis of the Mishnah advise us to judge everyone favorably[193] and to think positively about others. There is a very interesting story of Rabbi Israel Salanter, who related his own personal experience as follows:

"When I started to really serve God, I felt that everyone else was bad but I was good. Slowly, when I matured a bit more, I perceived that I was also bad. Eventually, I came to the conclusion that everyone else was good and I was bad." The truth is that we are the only ones who know our own failings. We should focus on them, and not on the failings of others. While thinking of ourselves positively and reviewing our successes, we have to also recognize and improve on our failures.

A great sage judged others: "If they were older than me, I would say that they must have done many more mitzvot than me. If they were younger than me, I would say that they had many fewer sins than me. About my contemporaries I would think that if they were more knowledgeable than me they were greater than me, and if they were less knowledgeable, then they were less guilty. This way, I always considered other people to be better than me.

The Talmud[194] also relates the story of Rabbi Shimon Bar Yochai and his son Rabbi Elazar. They hid from the Romans in a cave for twelve years, during which they spent their time learning Torah.

---

[192] Yoma 23a.

[193] Pirke Avot 1:6.

[194] Shabbat 33b.

When they came out of the cave, they became very angry when they found that no one was engaged in learning Torah but were engaged in mundane activities. They judged them harshly as being wasters of precious time. They were commanded by God to go back into their cave before they destroyed His world. When they came out a year later, their attitude had changed. They now realized that people engaged in necessary mundane activities could also be serving God.

Don't judge others until you are in their place.

5. Love Kindness

The prophet Micah (Chapter 10, Verse 8) sums up the 'bottom line' of the Torah:

"What does God require of you but to act justly, to love kindness and to walk humbly with your God?'

It seems that it is not enough to perform acts of kindness. One must learn to love acts of kindness. Obviously one should not say that "Since I am unable to perform this act with the proper motives, I will not do it at all." The Talmud says that a person should always do a good deed, even with the worst intentions, because good deeds have the intrinsic power to change the doer for the better. Eventually the person will come to appreciate the good deed and perform it with the right intentions.

6. Have Patience

Patience is one of the necessary ingredients for peace of mind and inner serenity. People should always be calm and patient, especially in their human relationships.

The Talmud, in Shabbat 31a, relates the story of Hillel the Elder, who was famous for his calm and unflappable nature. Two men wagered four hundred coins on whether one of them could make Hillel lose his temper.

The most harried time for religious Jews is on Friday afternoon, just before Shabbat, when last-minute preparations are in full swing. This was the time chosen as the most opportune to make Hillel lose his temper. Hillel was taking a bath when a stranger passed by his house, shouting "Is Hillel in? Is Hillel in?" Hillel wrapped himself in his bathrobe and came out of his house to greet him.

"What do you want, my son?" he calmly asked.

"I have a question for you." was the reply. The stranger asked a purposely silly question, to which Hillel gave a considered response. The man left seemingly satisfied, and Hillel returned to his bath.

The stranger returned twice more to ask other equally senseless questions, each time interrupting Hillel's Shabbat preparations. Hillel was not disturbed. He gave the man calm, measured responses and even praised him for the interesting questions that he had asked. Finally the man was nonplused and told Hillel that he had many more questions to ask him but was afraid that the sage would get angry. Hillel wrapped himself well and sat down, prepared for a long conversation, even though it was getting late. "Ask all the questions you want." said Hillel patiently.

"Are you Hillel, who people call the Prince of Israel?" The stranger asked.

"Yes." said Hillel.

"If so," said the man, "let there not be many people like you in Israel."

Hillel showed no sign of surprise at this statement, "My son, why?" was his only comment.

"Because you made me lose four hundred coins." was the angry response.

"Calm down." advised Hillel "it's better that you lose four hundred coins, than I should lose my temper."

The person who remains calm and cool will eventually win out in any situation, and will probably feel better and live longer as well.

Ten Guides to Success

You shall not worry, for worry is the most unproductive of all human activities.

You shall not be fearful, for most of the things we fear never come to pass.

You shall not attempt to cross bridges before you get to them, for no one yet has succeeded in accomplishing this.

You shall face each problem as it comes. You can handle only one at a time anyway.

You shall not take problems to bed with you, for they make very poor bedfellows.

You shall not borrow other people's problems. They can take better care of them than you can.

You shall not try to relive yesterday for good or ill. It is gone. Do teshuvah and move on. Concentrate on what is happening in your life today.

You shall count your blessings, never overlooking the small ones, for a lot of small blessings add up to a big one.

You shall be a good listener, for only when you listen do you hear ideas different from your own. It is very hard to learn something new when you are talking.

You shall not become bogged down by frustration, for 90 percent of it is rooted in self-pity and it will only interfere with positive action.

Chapter 9. Perfection

There are many aspects to perfection. Judaism, according to Rambam,[195] advocates a healthy soul in a healthy body. A healthy soul includes a healthy personality and a well-rounded character. In his treatise on the perfect personality[196] he has some extremely important insights for us, who are living in a generation that is probably the most reliant on psychologists, psychiatrists, and therapists ever.

Some of his major insights are: When people are physically sick, their taste buds usually do not work properly and they lose their sense of taste. For such a person, something that is really sweet may taste sour, and something that is really sour may taste sweet, so too in the world of the soul. A person who has a sick soul will have a desire for evil deeds, and someone with a healthy soul will have a desire for good deeds. Similarly, the personality of a person can become sick, and the worst character traits may rise to the surface.

Rambam defines for us a major principle in personality traits. It is called **'The Golden Mean'. A person should always take the medium path between the extreme positions of his or her personalities.** A person should not be so kind and generous that he or she gives away all their possessions. On the other hand, a person should not be so miserly that he or she does not give anything away. A person should not be so happy as to always break out in laughter for the slightest reason. On the other hand, a person should not be so serious that he or she is constantly in a depressed mood. A person must have a balance of being serious, yet happy and positive at the same time. Peace of mind is an integral part of perfection and is a prelude to happiness.

---

[195] Hilkhot De'ot Chapter 4:1.
[196] Hilkhot De'ot Chapter 2.

To understand what peace of mind and happiness are, let us first examine the opposite. Sadness results when a person does not have one of his or her basic human needs fulfilled. We find many cases of unhappy people at the beginning of the Torah: Adam, the Bible tells us, was lonely and not complete before Eve was formed. Eve was unhappy that she was not allowed to partake of the fruit of knowledge of good and evil. Cain was depressed when God did not accept his offering, but accepted his brother Abel's offering. Esau was unhappy when his blessing was stolen by his brother Jacob. Jacob was depressed when he thought that he had lost his beloved son Joseph forever.

With these primordial stories, the Torah teaches us about some of the causes of unhappiness.

- a. Desire for something that is forbidden or out of reach. (Adam for a partner; Eve for the fruit)
- b. Unsatisfied ego; societal recognition. (Cain)
- c. Loss of something precious. (Esau lost his blessing; Jacob lost his son, Joseph)
- d. Failure to live up to self-expectations; loss of self-respect. (Cain)
- e. Lack of purpose. (Eve)

Contentment in all these spheres is the key to peace of mind. I think that one of the most insightful and thought-provoking rabbinic statement is: "Who is a wealthy person? A person who is happy with his portion."[197]

As mentioned in a previous chapter, we consist of a 'quadrinity' of states: mental, emotional, spiritual, and physical, and we need to be in equilibrium to find peace. The Hebrew word for peace is Shalom, from the root 'Shalem,' which means completion or perfection. All our major prayers, the morning blessings, amidah,

---

[197] Pirke Avot 4:1.

and Birkat Hamazon, end with a prayer for peace. Peace is an ideal state that we all yearn for but which seems to be unattainable in this world, at least for now.

The Midrash,[198] states that Jacob, upon returning to Israel from his exile with his father-in-law, wanted to relax in peace and quiet. That is exactly when everything started to go wrong. His son Joseph disappeared.

In the Bible, all the great Jewish heroes seem to have imperfections. What unites them all is their striving toward a common goal - that of peace and perfection.

The role of a scholar, we say every day at the end of the morning prayers, is to increase peace in the world.

Joseph Albo, the famous medieval Spanish scholar and philosopher, made an interesting observation. "Peace is the harmony between two extremes. Peace (in our state of existence) is not the absence of strife." Peace of mind is the harmony between the extremes in our character. We have to balance the extreme forces in our character.

Worries do not give a person peace of mind. One technique to limit worries is to 'pass the buck.' We can pass the buck by transferring the burden of worry to our parents, the government, or ultimately to God.

Faith is a great cure for worry. There are some amusing anecdotes that illustrate this topic:

A person who was carrying a heavy backpack was waiting on the side of the road to hitch a ride with a passing vehicle. A car stopped for him and he got inside, but he kept his pack on his back. The

---

[198] Bereshit Raba 84.

driver asked him why he didn't unload his pack. The reply was "Well sir, it's enough that your car is carrying me. I don't want to trouble you to carry my backpack too!"

If God is carrying us anyway, why not give Him all our cares and troubles too?

Another story concerns a man who went to his Rabbi in desperation and asked for advice, "Rabbi, I have so many troubles - financial, health, family. What should I do?"

The Rabbi answered him "Go and speak to the janitor. He will advise you."

The janitor was destitute and of ill health. His teeth had fallen out at an early age. When the man found the janitor, he was baffled as to why the Rabbi sent him there, "What can the janitor teach me? He has enough problems of his own." Obeying the Rabbi's instructions, he asked the janitor what he did for his troubles.

"What troubles?" asked the janitor, "I don't have any!"

The lesson the Rabbi wanted him to learn was that even the worst situations in life can be looked at in a positive way. Even a person with terrible problems can survive without worry. It is all in one's mind.

Another story deals with a man who went to a Rabbi in desperation. "Rabbi, please pray for me." he begged, "I am in desperate need. I have so many troubles."

The Rabbi was not of much help. "I am afraid that my services don't come cheap. It will cost you $1000."
The man was shocked. There was no way that he could afford that. He pleaded with the Rabbi to do him a favor and pray for him

gratis. The Rabbi refused point blank, until the man said, "Rabbi, you know what? I don't need you. I'll pray for myself."

The Rabbi smiled in amusement and replied, "I was waiting for you to say that. We all have the ability to pray for ourselves, if only we used this ability."

It is extremely important to increase one's trust (bitachon) in God. The Torah[199] warns us not to forget that He is the one who gives us the ability to do great things. A person who truly has deep bitachon is radically different, in a positive way. If a person truly believed that God fixes his income from the beginning of the year, he wouldn't push himself so hard, or cut corners with the law and with other people in business. The Hafetz Haim gives a beautiful analogy to which this can be compared. A man is on a train and realizes that he will be late for his appointment in the next town. He runs to the front of the car and pushes the wall with all his might in an effort to make the train go faster. Sometimes, whatever we do, and however much we beat ourselves against the wall, nothing seems to go right. On the other hand, another person may be enjoying enormous material growth and prosperity with very little effort. As long as we tried our best, everything else is in God's hands.

Obviously we have to make our finest effort. We are not allowed to stand by foolishly and wait for miracles to happen.

The famous Bible commentator, Ramban, in Numbers 1:45, discusses the fact that Moses was commanded to count the men over twenty years of age. When a country prepares for war, it counts the able-bodied men. So too, the Jews were preparing to enter Israel and acted according to the ordinary rules of war. They did not rely on miracles, even though God had promised that one person would chase a thousand. This hammers home the message,

---

[199] Deuteronomy 8:18.

'Don't rely on miracles!'[200]

The classic example used to elaborate on this principle is that of Samuel the Prophet (1 Samuel 16:1) who, after King Saul's failure, was told by God to go to Bethlehem to anoint a new King from among the children of Jesse. Samuel's reaction is surprising. He questions God's command, saying "How can I go? If Saul hears [that I am anointing another King] he will kill me!"

God replied, "Take a calf with you, and say, 'I am coming to sacrifice to God.' Summon Jesse [to join] in the sacrificial meal, and I will tell you what to do. You will anoint for me the one I will designate."

The famous Bible commentator, the Radak,[201] emphasizes the importance the Torah attaches to allowing events to proceed in a 'natural' manner. Where dangers are prevalent and can reasonably be expected to occur, one should plan in advance to prevent a dangerous situation from developing, and avoid relying on God's miraculous intervention.[202]

Our Patriarch Jacob, for example, did not rely on miracles but prepared to meet his brother Esau with very practical measures. He sent gifts to Esau to pacify him. He split his camp in preparation for war and prayed to God for salvation.[203]

There is a story of a man who was caught in a storm where the whole town was flooding. This man had an immense faith in God,

---

[200] See also Numbers 13:2 and Rabbi Levi Ben Gershon - Ralbag on Samuel 2 Chapter 2 Verse 27.

[201] Acronym for Rabbi David Kimche 1157-1236, author of one of the most important commentaries on the Bible, which was first printed in the Mikraot Gedolot in Venice, 1517. The author, who lived in Narbonne, in southern France, sought to ascertain the precise meaning of the Biblical text. He also composed an important dictionary of Biblical word roots, entitled Sefer Hashorashim, in which he presented his interpretation of many verses not discussed in his commentary.

[202] Pesachim 8b.

[203] See Bereshit 32.

so when the police loudspeakers came around telling people to evacuate, he just laughed and continued with what he was doing. God would save him. When the boats came around looking for the stranded, he also laughed. He had perfect faith that God would save him. Finally the man was forced up to the roof of his home by the rising floodwater. Miraculously a helicopter came into view and the pilot spotted him, and, hovering above him, threw him a ladder. The man refused, saying that he has faith. Unfortunately the man drowned and went to heaven. "God, why didn't you save me? He asked in wonderment.

God replied, "I sent you the police, I sent the boat, and I sent the helicopter. Why didn't you get on?"

God sends us all sorts of messengers who offer us different opportunities. It is up to us to grab the opportunity and not let it pass. As the Talmud says, "God has many messengers." The classic story illustrating the idea that God has many messengers available to do his bidding is that of Elijah, who was running away from the wrath of Jezebel, and ran into the Negev Desert, totally depressed. God sent angels to feed him (1 Kings 19:5).

We are not allowed to rely solely on miracles. On the other hand, we are not allowed to cut corners either. We have to use all the legitimate means at our disposal to make a living and we should not shirk responsibility.

Rambam (Hilkhot De'ot 5:11) states this rule regarding the laws of marriage. 'The way of the wise is that first a person should earn a living, then acquire his own place to live, and only then get married. But fools first get married, and then if they can afford it, they acquire a place to live, and then at the end of their days they look for a trade or they are supported by charity.'

A person must find the golden mean between too much faith, relying on revealed miracles for survival, and too little faith, placing total reliance on his or her own self. The Torah[204] warns us not to fall in this latter trap to think that, 'my strength and the work of my hands made me all this wealth!'

The final ingredient for peace of mind is a clean conscience. Guilt is good, but only if it is acted upon to make changes and to repent. Teshuvah clears the conscience.

It is no coincidence that the last prayer before going to sleep at night is the Shema, where we accept on ourselves the unity and sovereignty of God. We entrust our care to His mercy. He watches over us while we sleep. This is a transfer of our cares and worries to Him. We also are meant to say viduy (confession) to repent for any wrongdoing during the previous day, and we forgive others for what they might have done to us. This enables us to clear our consciences before sleeping.

Many people today are afflicted with sleep disorders. Among the main reasons for this are that they have too many worries or that their consciences are not clear.

A person achieves happiness by finding the right partner. Like Adam, we all need somebody to complement our personality and to share life's joys and sorrows with. One must have a social framework to rely on, like a kind of safety net that supportive families usually provide.

One has to balance the different sides of his or her personality, finding self-respect in the process.

One has to be able to provide for his or her physical needs and necessities.

---

[204] Deuteronomy Chapter 8 verses 17,18.

One has to be able to channel his or her creative energies in the right direction and to try to realize his or her potential.

The following are essential for happiness: a sense of purpose or mission; a satisfying job; independence; helping others; imparting to others ethical monotheism; learning; self-improvement.

Faith and optimism are linked in the Jewish belief system. Fortunately, we have faith in a decent God who cares about our welfare and desires our benefit. When people face adversity in life, like David before and after he became King, they can turn to God and He answers their cry. Most of the Book of Psalms reflects David's entreaties to God in his times of trouble and despair.

Modern researchers today have proved that there is a correlation between praying and healing. Sick people who pray, heal faster and suffer fewer complications than those who don't pray. A person with faith in God will have a positive outlook in life.

The Jewish concept of the Messianic coming, based on our later prophets, especially Isaiah, Jeremiah and Zechariah, has served as a powerful tool to keep optimism alive in the face of incredible suffering and tremendous adversity. The final visions of our prophets are very optimistic and comforting. The ideas that eventually we will no longer be a scattered, persecuted remnant, that eventually there will be peace and brotherhood on earth, that no man shall lift their hands on their neighbors, are powerfully optimistic ones that have been adopted by the whole world. Witness the Isaiah Wall outside the UN building in New York. Rambam, nearly nine hundred years ago, pointed out how the whole Christian and Muslim world had adopted this Jewish concept of a Messiah and a Messianic era.

Notes

Chapter 10. The "Quick Reference Guide" to Inner Peace

The yearning of any normal, decent human being has to be for peace in one's life and in the world. In our morning prayers we say 'oseh shalom obere et hakol' - 'He makes peace and makes everything.' Rashi explains nothing is of value without peace. All Jewish prayers, the Morning Blessings, Amidah, and Birkat Hamazon, all end with a prayer for peace. Peace is an ideal state that we all yearn for but which seems to be unattainable in this world, at least for now. The Hebrew word for peace is Shalom, from the root 'Shalem,' which means completion or perfection. Judaism is an amazing system that builds from the ground up starting with the perfection of the individual and building into perfection of society. If all individuals are at peace within themselves and with others, society at large will have peace. The problem is that no one is taught how to be at peace within.

As mentioned in a previous chapter, we humans consist of a 'quadrinity' of states: mental, emotional, spiritual, and physical, and we need to harmonize and balance these qualities to be in equilibrium to find peace. We need to satisfy with moderation these four needs and make sure that our potential in these four areas is being met. Judaism advocates for a balanced existence. In his treatise on the perfect personality Rambam advocates a healthy soul in a healthy body. A healthy soul includes a healthy personality and a well-rounded character.

Mental: People need to find an occupation or hobby that is mentally stimulating that will make them think and use their brains. I highly advocate learning Torah especially mussar (ethics); halakhah (Jewish Law) and Jewish History to know our roots and the messages of our prophets.

Emotional: We all need social outlets: parents; spouse; children; community. We need to love and be loved. A person achieves happiness by finding the right partner. Like Adam, we all need somebody to complement our personality and to share life's joys and sorrows with. One must have a social framework to rely on, like a kind of safety net that supportive families usually provide.

Spiritual: Pray to God, reach out to Him, connect, commune, and meditate daily or better thrice daily according to Jewish ritual. Our Creator is our King; our Father; our friend and companion who is reachable 24/7 to whom we can unburden our problems anytime. If you need a spiritual boost any time of day, read and sing Psalms of King David (Tehillim). Do what is right in God's Law (the Torah). Live with optimism: faith and optimism are linked in the Jewish belief system. Fortunately, we have faith in a decent God who cares about our welfare and desires our benefit. Modern researchers today have proved that there is a correlation between praying and healing. Sick people who pray heal faster and suffer fewer complications than those who don't pray. A person with faith in God will have a positive outlook on life.   ·

Physical: Exercise; eat healthful food; no drugs, booze, smoking or gambling. Eat right and sleep right: six to eight hours a night. Live a moral lifestyle, no sex outside marriage; monogamy is good for the health and morality.[205] A major survey of 127,545 American adults found that married men are healthier than men who were never married or whose marriages ended in divorce or widowhood. Men who have marital partners also live longer than

---

[205] STDs are a significant health challenge facing the United States. CDC estimates that nearly 20 million new sexually transmitted infections occur every year in this country, half among young people ages 15–24. Each of these infections is a potential threat to an individual's immediate and long-term health and well-being. In addition to increasing a person's risk for HIV infection, STDs can lead to severe reproductive health complications, such as infertility and ectopic pregnancy. STDs are also a serious drain on the U.S. health care system, costing the nation almost $16 billion in health care costs every year. http://www.cdc.gov/nchhstp/newsroom/docs/STD-Trends-508.pdf

men without spouses; and the longer a man stays married, the greater his survival advantage over his unmarried peers.[206]

Personality: We are the sum total of our personality traits and we need to 'tune' up our traits so that our lives will run smoother, better and more successfully. Our goal in Personality Development is 'The Golden Mean', the medium path between the extreme positions of our personalities. One has to balance the different sides of his or her personality, finding self-esteem in the process. One has to be able to channel his or her creative energies in the right direction and to try to realize his or her potential.

The Torah teaches us about some of the causes of unhappiness:

   a. Desire for something that is forbidden or out of reach.
   b. Unsatisfied ego; societal recognition.
   c. Loss of something precious.
   d. Failure to live up to self-expectations; loss of self-respect.
   e. Lack of purpose.
   f. Worries do not give a person peace of mind.

One technique to limit worries is to 'pass the buck.' We can pass the buck by transferring the burden of worry to our parents, the government, or ultimately to God. Faith is a great cure for worry.

If God is carrying us anyway, why not give Him all our cares and troubles too?

Obviously we have to make our finest effort. We are not allowed to stand by foolishly and wait for miracles to happen. 'Don't rely on miracles!'

---

[206] www.health.harvard.edu/newsletters/Harvard_Mens_Health_Watch/2010/July/marriage-and-mens-health

God sends us all sorts of messengers who offer us different opportunities. It is up to us to grab the opportunity and not let it pass.

The following are essential for happiness:

1. **A sense of purpose or mission**

2. **A satisfying job, or mission, or hobby**

3. **Independence**

4. **Helping others**

5. **Imparting to others ethical monotheism**

6. **Learning**

7. **Self-improvement**

8. **Friendship**

9. **Loving and being loved**

10. **Optimism**

11. **Faith in God**

The Jewish concept of the Messianic coming, based on our later prophets, especially Isaiah, Jeremiah and Zechariah, has served as a powerful tool to keep optimism alive in the face of incredible suffering and tremendous adversity.

The final visions of our prophets are very optimistic and comforting. Things <u>will</u> get better; and the world <u>will</u> become a better place.

Glossary

<u>Rambam, Rabbi Moses Ben Maimon</u> also known as Maimonides, was born in Cordova, Spain in 1138, and died in Egypt in 1204. After Spain was invaded by a fanatic Muslim tribe from North Africa, Rambam's family went into exile, and eventually settled in Fez, Morocco in 1160. Even during these difficult years, Rambam was already creating the books that eventually earned him international fame. His commentary on the Mishnah, in Arabic, was among the first of these works. In Fez, Rambam also studied medicine, and later he earned his livelihood as a physician. In 1165, his entire family left Morocco and moved to Israel, although subsequent difficulties forced the family to leave Israel for Egypt. After the death of Rambam's father, the family settled in Fostat (old Cairo). Rambam's multi-faceted activities included serving as chief rabbi, head of the rabbinical court, and head of the Jewish community. In addition, he taught, wrote, and served as personal physician to the sultan Saladin. Rambam was familiar with every branch of contemporary science and philosophy and every realm of Jewish knowledge - Talmud and halachah, philosophy and ethics. He penned hundreds of responsa to queries from throughout the Jewish world. He also authored the Guide to the Perplexed, a philosophical treatise that attempts to reconcile Jewish belief with contemporary philosophy. Many of the philosophical concepts in this work were considered highly controversial. Rambam also authored Mishneh Torah (the "second Torah," also known as Yad Ha-Chazakah - The Strong Hand. The gematriah, or numerical value of the word for hand in Hebrew, yad is fourteen, corresponding to the fourteen sections of his book.), which summarizes the entire oral law clearly, concisely, and in organized fashion. In many communities, particularly among Yemenite Jews, the Mishneh Torah was accepted as halachically authoritative.

Another work by Rambam, Sefer Hamitzvot, lists the 613 commandments and presents systematic criteria for the enumeration of these commandments.

Ramban, Rabbi Moses Ben Nachman, also known as Nachmanides, was born in Gerona, Spain in 1194, and died in Israel in 1270. Ramban was the outstanding Torah authority of his generation. His multifaceted literary activities included commentaries on the Bible and Talmud, halachic codes, responsa, works on mysticism and philosophy, and sermons. When he moved to Israel in his old age, Ramban restored the Jewish community in Jerusalem, which had previously been destroyed by invading Tartars. Accordingly, Ramban is considered the father of modern Jewish settlement in Jerusalem. Like Maimonides and many other Spanish rabbinic scholars, Ramban was a practicing physician.

Rashi, Rabbi Shlomo Yitzhaki, the eleventh century French Biblical commentator, was born in Troyes, France in 1040, and died in Worms, Germany in 1105. He studied in the yeshivot of Troyes, Mainz, and Worms. His teachers, Rabbi Jacob ben Yakar and Rabbi Isaac ben Judah, were students of Rabbenu Gershon Me'or Ha-Golah (q.v.). In 1070, Rashi founded his Yeshivah in Troyes, which was attended by students from far and near. Rashi had no sons, but his daughters' sons included such illustrious scholars as: Rabbenu Tam and Rashbam, both of whom were among the founders of the Franco-German Tosafist school of Talmud study. Rashi wrote commentaries on the Bible and the Talmud, which are considered indispensable for the study of these works.

Dessler, Rabbi Eliyahu, 1891-1954, Rabbi Dessler was born into a family steeped in the Mussar movement, founded by Rabbi Israel Salanter. Most of his education took place in Kelm. In 1929 he became a Rabbi in London and in 1941 he accepted the directorship of the Gateshead Kollel. In the 1950's he moved to Israel, where he was appointed mashgiach (guidance counselor) of Ponevich Yeshivah. His essays have been collected in four volumes under the title Strive for Truth.

DEDICATION

This book is dedicated in loving memory of our parents

Florence and David I. Goldberg z"l

יצחק דוד בן גרשון ז׳׳ל, צפורה בת נחמיה שמואל ז׳׳ל

As community leaders in Fair Lawn and Bergen County, New Jersey, they worked tirelessly to promote Jewish education and unity.

And in memory of our son and nephew

David Yitzchak Cohen z"l

דוד יצחק בן אברהם ושרון הכהן ז׳׳ל

David packed a huge amount of living and learning into his 33 short years. He was passionate about studying Torah, physics and math as the means of understanding Hashem's creation and engaging in tikkun olam.

ת.נ.צ.ב.ה.

Avi and Sharon Cohen
Gershon Goldberg
Michael and Judy Goldrich

If you would like to participate in the
mitzvah of printing more copies of this
or other volumes
please contact Rabbi Bassous at
bassous@yahoo.com